Simple Recipes for Stylish Jewellery

Over 80 Projects

Stephanie Burnham, Amanda Walker,
Helen Birmingham, Michelle Bungay,
Sarah Lawrence and Suzen Millodot

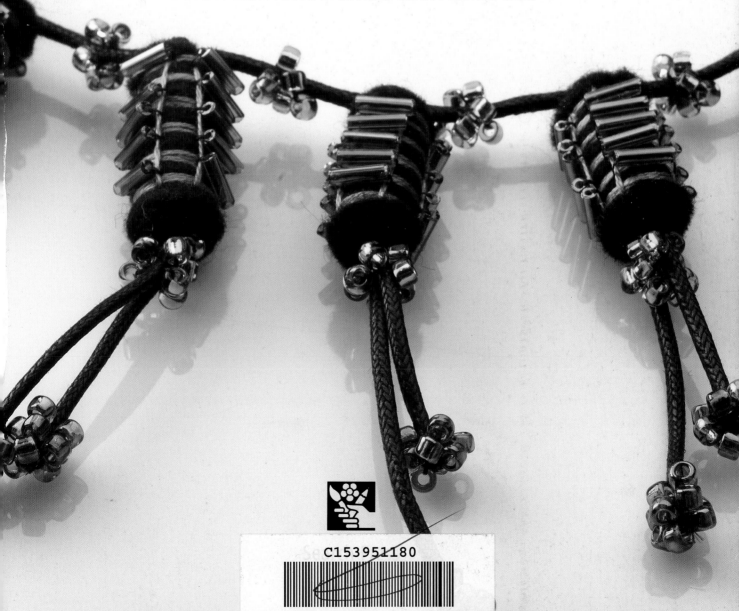

First published in Great Britain 2010

Search Press Limited
Wellwood, North Farm Road,
Tunbridge Wells, Kent TN2 3DR

Based on the following books published by Search Press:
Twenty to Make: Bracelets by Amanda Walker (2007)
Twenty to Make: Beaded Felt Jewellery by Helen Birmingham (2008)
Twenty to Make: Charms by Stephanie Burnham (2007)
Twenty to Make: Necklaces by Stephanie Burnham (2007)
Twenty to Make: Tiaras & Hairpins by Michelle Bungay (2008)
Twenty to Make: Wild Women by Sarah Lawrence (2008)
Twenty to Make: Micro Macramé Jewellery by Suzen Millodot (2009)

Text copyright © Stephanie Burnham, Amanda Walker, Helen Birmingham,
Michelle Bungay, Sarah Lawrence and Suzen Millodot, 2010

Photographs by Roddy Paine Photographic Studio (pages 30–55) and
Debbie Patterson at Search Press Studios and on location (pages 1–29, 56–192)

Photographs and design copyright © Search Press Ltd 2010

ISBN: 978-1-84448-533-8

Suppliers
If you have difficulty in obtaining any of the materials and equipment
mentioned in this book, then please visit the Search Press website for
details of suppliers: www.searchpress.com

Printed in Malaysia.

Contents

Bracelets

by Amanda Walker

Making bracelets is a great introduction to the craft of jewellery-making. Simply link a few beautiful beads together, attach a fastening and there you have it!

Very little equipment needs to be purchased – in fact, you may find you already have a couple of pairs of pliers and a wire cutter, and these are all the tools that you will need.

It may help if you think of bracelets as tiny necklaces. Both use the same design methods but the finished article will take half the time, which in our time-starved society can only be a good thing. You wait and see; once you have made one there will be no stopping you as your confidence soars and your techniques develop.

I find that each bracelet I make gives me new ideas that I can use on other bracelets or even in other areas of jewellery-making. Go on – have a go at making one of these beautiful bracelets.

A variety of beautiful bracelets that you can make using the techniques shown in this chapter.

A note on beads:

There is a vast array of beautiful beads available on the market and it can be confusing working out exactly which sort you need.

Beads and all related products such as findings (all the pieces needed to connect and assemble the jewellery; e.g. head and eye pins and fastenings) are becoming more readily available as the jewellery-making craft is growing. These are generally sold in the haberdashery department of a store or in specialist craft shops.

Beads are sold in metric measurements which give the diameter of the bead: e.g. 6mm glass pearl. Smaller beads are generally sold by weight in grams, while larger beads are available separately or in multiple packs.

Do look at the size of the threading hole and check that the beading elastic or thread is the right weight to fit through the holes. Some handmade glass beads have very large holes, but if you use a smaller bead (such as a rocaille) on either side this will help to position the bead correctly on the thread or elastic. Conversely some pearls have very small holes and the weight of thread or elastic must be adjusted to suit.

It is essential to use beading needles as the holes in the small rocaille beads are tiny and the eye of a general sewing needle would be too large. Beading needles come in different lengths depending on what kind of beading you are doing. I generally find longer needles to be preferable.

Sea Bride

Materials:

11 x green handmade glass beads
11 x silver eye pins
1 x decorative ring and bar clasp
2 x silver jump rings

Tools:

Flat-nosed pliers
Half round-nosed pliers
Wire cutters

Instructions:

1 Thread a glass bead on to an eye pin. Using flat-nosed pliers bend the wire to a right angle and then cut, leaving 1cm (³/₈in) of wire above the bead.

2 Using the round-nosed pliers bend the wire into a loop. Just before closing the loop fully, thread on another eye pin, then repeat this process ten more times.

3 Finally, attach a jump ring to the last eye pin, then attach the ring and bar clasp to each end of the linked beads.

Devotion
This bracelet was made using the same techniques with metal beads in place of the glass ones.

Love-me-knot

Materials:

50cm (20in) black leather lacing

1 x green luena glass bead

Tools:

Scissors

Instructions:

1 Form the lacing into a double circle. Wrap the right-hand end loosely over the doubled lacing three times, then thread the end back through the wrapped section. Pull the end tight to make a knot (see inset opposite).

2 Thread a luena bead on to the left-hand lacing end, then make a second knot by wrapping the left-hand end loosely under the doubled lacing three times, with the end pulled in the opposite direction, approximately 10cm (4in) away from the first.

3 Trim away any excess lacing with the scissors. The knots are slip knots, making the bracelet easy to adjust to fit your wrist.

Forget-me-knot

This bracelet uses a blue luena bead for a simple alternative.

Attraction

Materials:

6 x 8mm round magnetic beads

106 x 4mm aqua faceted glass beads

4 x silver headpins

2 x eye pins

2 x calottes

50cm (20in) nylon transparent thread
  (0.25mm diameter)

Tools:

Flat-nosed pliers

Half round-nosed pliers

Wire cutters

Scissors

Beading needle

Jewellery glue

Instructions:

1 Thread the needle with the transparent thread and tie a knot approximately 10cm (4in) from the end of the beading thread.

2 Thread on forty faceted beads, then tie a knot close to the beads and cut the thread leaving a 10cm (4in) tail. Repeat the process with a second length of thread.

3 Put the two beaded threads next to each other, then pass one end of each of the threads through a single faceted bead and a calotte. Tie a few knots and dot with glue to secure the beaded thread, then close the calotte. Repeat at the other end with another faceted bead and calotte.

4 Thread two eye pins with three magnetic and one faceted bead each, then thread four headpins with six faceted beads each.

5 Using flat-nosed pliers bend the pins at right angles, then cut, leaving 1cm (³/₈in) of pin above the beads. Using the round-nosed pliers, bend the pin ends into loops.

6 Attach two threaded headpins to the two eye pins, then the eye pins to the calottes.

Hollywood Starlet
Simply substitute white beads for the blue beads to make this glamorous bracelet.

Opulence

Materials:

200cm (79in) of light blue nylon thread

10 x 6mm tanzanite (grey) faceted glass beads

25cm (10in) of silver fine chain

4 x 4mm silver jump rings

2 x silver end caps

24 x silver crimp beads

10mm silver lobster clasp

Tools:

Flat-nosed pliers

Half round-nosed pliers

Crimping pliers

Wire cutters

Scissors

Jewellery glue

Instructions:

1 Cut eight 20cm (7¾in) lengths of nylon thread. Take two lengths and thread a crimp bead on to join them. Anchor the crimp bead in place with the crimping pliers, then thread on a faceted bead and position it with the crimp bead.

2 Slip another crimp bead on to the lengths and crimp it in place, sandwiching the bead.

3 Use crimp beads to secure two more beads along the pair of threads to complete the length.

4 Make one more nylon thread pair in the same way with three beads, and two pairs with two beads.

5 Glue the ends of the four pairs of beaded threads together, then encase them inside the end caps.

6 Loosely wrap the chain around the threads. Attach jump rings to the end caps and chain ends and then attach the lobster clasp.

Purity

Using lime green glass pearls and changing the colour of the other materials can create a very different effect. Try changing the number of beads (as shown below) for another simple variation.

Illusion

Materials:

6 x 16mm black wrapped beads

27 x 10mm steel glass pearls

70 x 4mm half silver crystal faceted glass beads

44cm (17¾in) of platinum fine chain

1 x silver spring fastening

1 x silver extension chain with heart

4 x silver jump rings

2 x 4mm silver end caps

100cm (36in) of 0.25mm nylon
   transparent thread

Tools:

Flat-nosed pliers

Half round-nosed pliers

Wire cutters

Scissors

Beading needle

Jewellery glue

Instructions:

1 Thread the needle with the transparent thread and tie a knot approximately 10cm (4in) from the end. Thread on fifty faceted beads, tie a knot close to the beads to secure them and then cut the thread leaving a 10cm (4in) tail.

2 Take another length of thread, tie a knot 10cm (4in) from the end and thread on a faceted glass bead, then twenty glass pearls and then another faceted glass bead. Tie a knot close to the bead and cut the thread, leaving a 10cm (4in) tail.

3 Thread a third length with the remaining faceted beads, alternating glass pearls and wrapped beads between pairs of faceted beads.

4 Pass all three threads through a single faceted bead, tie in a knot, place a dot of glue on the knot and encase in an end cap. Repeat on the other end.

5 Cut the chain in half and attach in two strands to the jump rings; attach the rings behind the single faceted beads.

6 Attach jump rings to the end caps, then the fastening and extension chain.

Neptune's Treasure

Using copper materials rather than silver, and ivory rather than black wrapped beads will give you a bracelet with a vintage style.

Eastern Princess

Materials:

36cm (14in) of 3.5cm (1¼in) wide ivory
  transparent ribbon
7 x silver drum eye divider beads
6 x silver ring diamond divider beads
3 x salmon (pink) luena glass beads
4 x handmade glass beads
6 x 6mm silver round fantasy metal beads
8 x 4mm silver crystal faceted glass beads
2 x 6mm silver end caps
9 x 4mm silver jump rings
1 x horseshoe-shaped ring and bar clasp
7 x headpins

Tools:

Flat-nosed pliers
Half round-nosed pliers
Wire cutters
Scissors

Instructions:

1 Cut the ribbon into two 18cm (7in) lengths and hold the lengths together. Starting with a drum eye divider bead, thread on seven drum eye metal divider beads, alternating them with six ring diamond divider beads.

2 Gather both ends of the ribbon and encase them in the end caps, then attach jump rings.

3 Attach the horseshoe ring and bar clasp to the jump rings.

4 Thread a headpin with a faceted bead, a handmade glass bead and another faceted bead. Repeat with three more headpins.

5 Thread a headpin with a round metal bead, a salmon luena bead and another metal bead. Repeat with two more headpins. Using flat-nosed pliers, bend the wires at right angles, then cut, leaving 1cm ($^3/_8$in) of wire above the beads.

6 Using the round-nosed pliers, bend the wires into loops and attach these to the drum eye beads with jump rings.

Butterfly

Rather than use headpins, you can simply attach butterfly charms to the drum divider beads using jump rings.

Egypt

Materials:

5 x turquoise wrapped 16mm beads

10 x 16mm bead caps

10 x 4mm aqua faceted glass beads

5 x eye pins

5cm (2in) of fine gold chain

1 x gold extension chain with heart
and lobster clasp

Tools:

Flat-nosed pliers

Half round-nosed pliers

Wire cutters

Instructions:

1 Put two bead caps on one of the turquoise wrapped beads, then thread it on to an eye pin between two faceted beads (see detail opposite).

2 Using flat-nosed pliers, bend the wire to a right angle and then cut, leaving 1cm (³⁄₈in) of pin above the beads. Using the round-nosed pliers, bend the wire into a loop. Just before closing the loop fully, thread on another eye pin prepared in the same way.

3 Repeat this process five times.

4 Cut two 2.5cm (1in) lengths of chain using the wire cutters. Open the loop of the eye pin at each end and attach the chain.

5 Open the last link of each piece of chain and attach the lobster clasp and the extension chain.

Orient

For this opulent black bracelet, thread on 6mm gold metal beads instead of the faceted beads.

Cool Mint Knots

Materials:

56cm (22in) of black leather lacing

4 x green glass handmade beads

2 x silver metal beads

1 x pendant metal bead

12 x 2mm silver-lined clear rocailles

8 x 4mm silver jump rings

1 x 8mm silver jump rings

2 x 6mm silver end caps

6 x headpins

1 x silver spring fastening

Tools:

Flat-nosed pliers

Half round-nosed pliers

Wire cutters

Scissors

Instructions:

1 Cut the leather lacing in half and hold the two halves together. Using them as one strand, make a loop and take the free ends over and through the loop to make a knot near the middle.

2 Tie a second knot 2.5cm (1in) from the other, taking the free ends under and through the loop to make a knot that faces the other way (see detail opposite). Encase both sets of free ends in the end caps.

3 Attach two 4mm jump rings and then the spring fastening to the end caps.

4 Thread four handmade glass beads and two metal beads on to separate heads pins, threading a rocaille on each side of the beads.

5 Using flat-nosed pliers, bend the pins at right angles then cut them, leaving 1cm (³⁄₈in) of wire above the beads.

6 Use the round-nosed pliers to bend the wires into loops. Attach the 8mm jump ring to the metal pendant bead to make a pendant.

7 Divide the threaded headpins into two groups, with two glass beads and one metal bead in each group. Thread each group on to a separate jump ring.

8 Link two jump rings together, attaching the assembled jump rings to each end. Link another jump ring to one end and then attach this ring to the leather lacing between the knots, with the remaining metal bead attached to it with the final jump ring.

Fly-by-night
Made in exactly the same way as the bracelet opposite, dusky pink tanzanite beads replace the green glass beads in this variation.

Trueheart

Materials:

1 x copper metal bracelet
6 x metal copper hearts
28 x 4mm metal bronze faceted glass beads
13 x copper headpins

Tools:

Flat-nosed pliers
Half round-nosed pliers
Wire cutters

Instructions:

1 Thread six headpins with the copper hearts, then bend the pins at right angles using flat-nosed pliers. Cut the wire, leaving 1cm (³/₈in) above the beads.

2 Using the round-nosed pliers, bend the wires into loops.

3 Thread seven headpins with four faceted bronze beads each (see detail opposite). Bend, cut and loop the ends of the pins in the same way as the pins with hearts.

4 Thread these assembled headpins alternately on to the copper bracelet.

Opulence

This variation uses single decorative beads in place of the faceted bronze beads. In addition, the metal flowers and decorative beads are sandwiched between rocailles.

Silver Zephyr

Materials:

9 x assorted handmade blue glass iris beads

7 x silver metal dot-patterned divider drum beads

6 x silver metal diamond-patterned divider ring beads

1 x open cross charm

2 x 6mm silver metal fantasy round beads

3 x silver headpins

4 x 8mm silver jump rings

20cm (7¾in) of nylon transparent elastic

20cm (7¾in) of 0.25mm nylon transparent thread

Tools:

Flat-nosed pliers

Half round-nosed pliers

Wire cutters

Scissors

Beading needle

Jewellery glue

Instructions:

1 Thread a beading needle with a short length of thread, double over and tie the two ends in a knot. Pass the needle through one of the metal beads, leaving a loop of thread on the other side of the bead.

2 Thread the elastic into this loop and then pull the needle and thread fully through the bead which in turn pulls the elastic through as well. Thread the seven glass and the thirteen metal beads using the photograph opposite as a guide.

3 Knot the two ends of the elastic firmly together, placing a dot of glue on to the knot.

4 Thread two headpins with the remaining glass beads. Using flat-nosed pliers bend the pins at right angles, then cut, leaving 1cm (³/₈in) of wire above the beads.

5 Thread the last headpin with the last drum bead sandwiched between the two 6mm metal fantasy round beads. Using flat-nosed pliers bend the pins at right angles, then cut, leaving 1cm (³/₈in) of wire above the beads.

6 Using the round-nosed pliers bend the wires into loops. Attach a jump ring to each of the prepared headpins and one to the metal cross charm.

7 Attach the jump rings to the elastic between the metal beads (see detail opposite).

Genie
Handmade glass beads make distinctive jewellery because of their unique shapes.

Rose Pearls

Materials:

18cm (7in) heavy silver chain
1 x large silver ring and bar clasp
8 x 12mm dusky pink glass pearls
8 x silver headpins

Tools:

Flat-nosed pliers
Half round-nosed pliers
Wire cutters

Instructions:

1 Open out the last links on the ends of the chain and attach them to the ring and bar clasp.

2 Thread eight headpins with the glass pearls. Use flat-nosed pliers to bend the pins at right angles, then use the wire cutters to trim them, leaving 1cm (³⁄₈in) of wire above the beads.

3 Thread a pin end through a link on the chain and then use the round-nosed pliers to bend the wire into a loop.

4 Repeat this process with the remaining seven threaded pins, spacing the beads evenly along the chain.

Harvest
Olive green pearls give a restful, natural look to this bracelet.

Reflection

Materials:

9 x silver rings with two eyes

9 x 6mm aqua faceted glass beads

18 x silver lined rocailles

9 x silver eye pins

2 x silver jump rings

1 x bow-and-arrow ring and bar clasp

Tools:

Flat-nosed pliers

Half round-nosed pliers

Wire cutters

Instructions:

1 Thread an eye pin through the first hole of a silver ring, then thread a rocaille, glass bead and rocaille on to the eye pin before taking the pin through the second hole of the silver ring.

2 Using flat-nosed pliers, bend the pin to a right angle and then cut the pin with wire cutters, leaving 1cm (³/₈in) of wire above the ring and bead.

3 Using the round-nosed pliers, bend the pin into a loop. Just before closing the loop fully, thread on another eye pin and repeat this sequence of rings and beads eight more times.

4 Attach a jump ring to each end and then the ring and bar clasp to the jump rings.

Ardent Truth

The diamond flower beads used below fit the silver rings perfectly.

29

Beaded Felt Jewellery

by Helen Birmingham

In this chapter I will show you how you can use the humble felt square to create sophisticated and fashionable felt jewellery without the need for specialist materials or wet, soapy hands!

All the designs are based around eight simple methods for binding and decorating felt beads, and these are shown on pages 32–33. As you will see, the overall effect of these beads is stunning, yet the technique to make them could not be easier!

I use bright colours and bold designs for maximum impact – be inspired by them, and adapt them to suit your own personal taste or style.

A friend once told me that my jewellery was as exciting as a sweet shop – but without the calories! I hope you will find this collection of necklaces, bracelets and earrings equally as delicious, and that it will whet your appetite for creating gorgeous designs of your own.

These fantastic pieces of beaded felt jewellery show the results you can get using the techniques shown in this chapter.

Methods

All the beads I have used are based around the principle of rolling a piece of felt tightly around a stick and binding it with thread to form a bead. I find that bamboo sticks are ideal as they are very smooth and uniform in size, but wooden skewers, cocktail sticks or even thin knitting needles work just as well. Avoid using drinking straws, because you may stitch through the straw when adding decoration and then be unable to remove the bead!

As with all handmade beads, slight irregularities in size and shape are welcomed and it is not vital that the felt pieces are cut to exact measurements, but I would recommend that all the felt pieces for one project are cut at the same time. Keep the finished beads on the stick until you are ready to use them – without the stick they flatten easily and you can end up losing the hole!

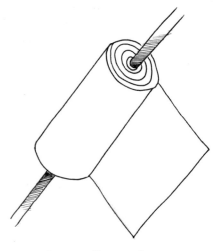

Basic rolling technique

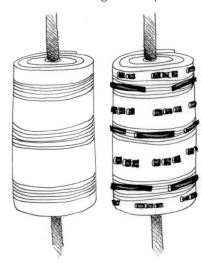

Method A

Making the felt beads

The best way to wrap the thread is to thread a needle and knot the end. Roll the felt around the stick, already having threaded and knotted the thread. Holding the roll in place with one hand, pass the needle down into the bead next to the cocktail stick and bring it out again part way along the length of the bead, thus hiding the knot in the middle of the bead. Hold the roll in place while you bind and decorate the bead by either simply holding it or adding a small amount of fabric glue. Fasten off with a couple of small stitches, one on top of the other. Pass the needle back into the bead and out again at the top next to the stick and cut off end of thread.

To secure the beads and stitching lengthwise on the bead, make sure you keep the bead on the stick! Attach thread as above, making sure this time that the thread is coming out at the far end of the bead. Then load up the thread with the required seed beads and pass the needle back into the top of the felt bead, effectively making one long stitch (containing the seed beads) along the whole length of the felt bead. Continue as necessary.

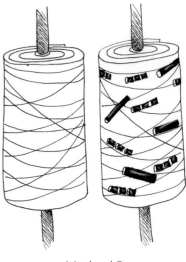

Method B

Method C

Method D

Method E

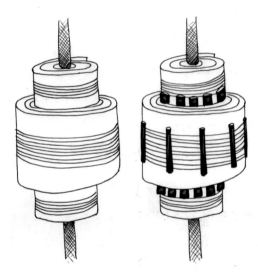

Method F

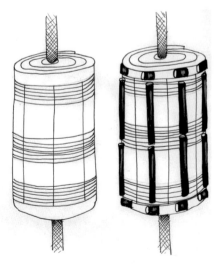

Method G

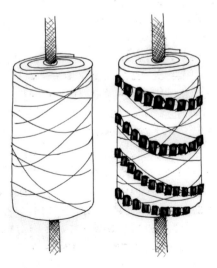

Method H

33

Sweet Peanut Bracelet

Materials:
6 x tan felt pieces, 2.5 x 6cm (1 x 2¼in)
6 x yellow wooden spacer beads
Selection of gold/yellow seed beads
Selection of gold/yellow bugle beads
Tan embroidery thread
Beading thread
Round elastic

Tools:
Scissors
Beading needle
Needle

Instructions:

1 Bind the felt pieces into six beads using embroidery thread and attach seed beads and bugle beads, following method A.

2 Thread felt beads and spacer beads alternately on to the elastic.

3 Tie a knot securely in the elastic, keeping the elastic taut but not fully stretched.

4 Cut off the ends of the elastic close to the knot.

5 Gently pull the elastic through one of the felt beads, so that the knot sits invisibly within the bead.

34

Turkish Delight

*Use passionate pinks and purples to create a bracelet
hot enough to sizzle on a night full of Eastern Promise.*

Cola Drops

Materials:

2 x orange-coloured felt pieces, 2.5 x 6cm (1 x 2¼in)

4 x flat black spacer beads

4 x small gold beads

2 x headpins

2 x long ball wire earring hooks

Selection of gold/yellow seed beads

Selection of gold/yellow bugle beads

Tan embroidery thread

Beading thread

Tools:

Round-nose pliers

Flat-nose pliers

Cutting pliers

Scissors

Beading needle

Needle

Instructions:

1 Bind the felt pieces into two beads using embroidery thread and attach seed beads and bugle beads, following method A.

2 Thread beads on to a headpin in the following order – small gold bead, flat black spacer, felt bead, flat black spacer and small gold bead.

3 Snip the headpin to length and create a loop. You need to leave about 1cm (³/₈in) of headpin above the beading to form the loop.

4 Attach an earring hook to the loop.

5 Repeat for the second earring.

Raspberry Drops

This colour scheme matches the Turkish Delight bracelet on page 35. Making matching earrings is a simple and subtle way of coordinating your outfit.

Liquorice Whip

Materials:

15 x black felt pieces, 2.5 x 6cm (1 x 2¼in)
A selection of black seed beads
A selection of black bugle beads
Black embroidery thread
Beading thread
Medium cotton cord
2 x round leather crimps
1 x sprung hook

Tools:

Scissors
Flat-nose pliers
Beading needle
Needle

Instructions:

1 Bind the felt pieces into fifteen beads using embroidery thread and attach seed beads and bugle beads, following method A.

2 Thread the felt beads on to the cord.

3 Knot the cord securely at each end of the beading. This prevents the fastening from moving round to the front when you are wearing the necklace.

4 Add more knots for decoration.

5 Cut the ends of the cord to the desired length.

6 Attach a leather crimp to each cut end of the cord.

7 Attach the hook to one of the crimps.

Rhubarb and Custard

For a complete change from the dark sophistication of the black necklace, try using a combination of pinks and yellows to make a lighter, more summery necklace.

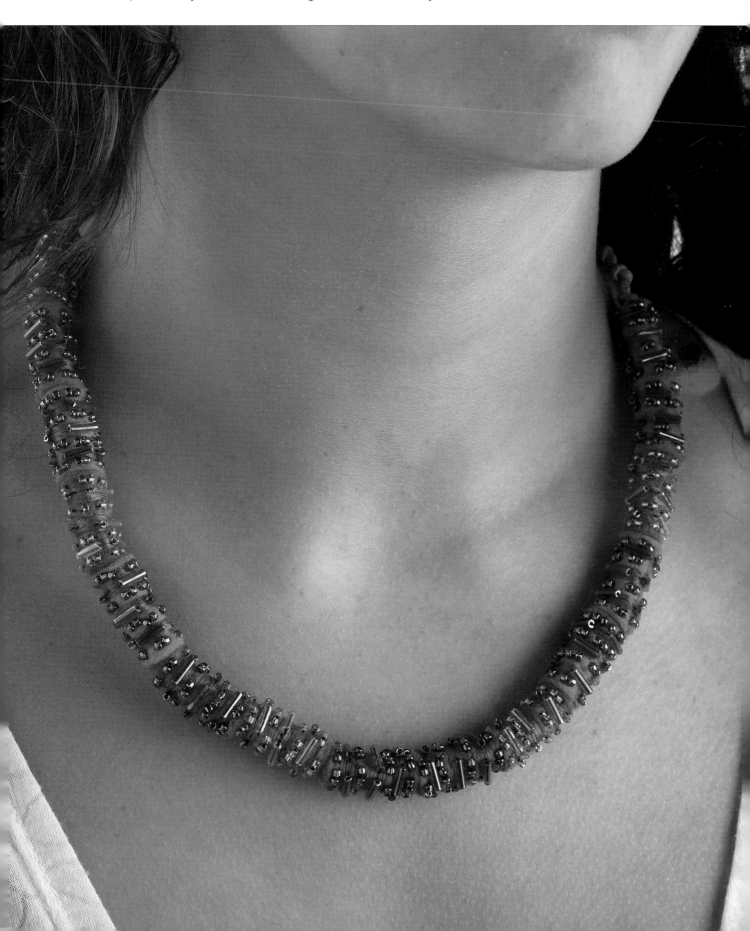

Peppermint Moss Bangle

Materials:

8 x green felt pieces, 2.5 x 8cm (1 x 3¼in)

Selection of iridescent green seed beads

Selection of iridescent green bugle beads

Copper-coloured sparkly embroidery thread

Beading thread

Medium cotton cord

Tools:

Scissors

Beading needle

Needle

Instructions:

1 Bind the felt pieces into eight beads using embroidery thread, following method B.

2 Thread the felt beads on to the cord and knot the cord securely to form a bangle. This will make a fixed-size bangle, so ensure the size is correct before continuing. If the bangle needs to be larger, add a ninth felt bead.

3 Carefully position the knot inside one of the felt beads.

4 Using embroidery thread, darn the ends of the felt beads together using stab stitches. (Be aware that you will need to lengthen the stitches to accommodate the outside curve of the bangle.)

5 Stitch bugle beads over the join to decorate.

6 Add a string of seed beads, twisting and turning it around the felt beads and anchoring it every now and then by stab stitching directly through the cord.

Forget-me-not

This bangle would make a perfect gift for a sister or mother. Cool blue teamed with silver is a timeless combination.

Mango Cluster

Materials:

8 x red felt pieces, 2.5 x 8cm (1 x 3¼in)
Selection of iridescent bronze seed beads
Selection of iridescent bronze bugle beads
Soft orange embroidery thread
2 x lengths of medium cotton cord
Beading thread

Tools:

Scissors
Beading needle
Needle

Instructions:

1 Bind the felt pieces into eight beads using embroidery thread and attach seed beads, following method G.

2 Thread one felt bead on to the first cord and position it at the centre of the cord.

3 Secure this bead in place by stab stitching directly into the cord using beading thread.

4 Stitch seed beads directly on to the cord to form clusters. Use ten seed beads for each cluster and leave a gap of about 1cm (³/₈in) between each cluster and felt bead.

5 Repeat by threading felt beads and creating clusters until you have five beads and six clusters stitched into place on the cord.

6 Tie a sliding knot on to the cord, and decorate the cut ends with seed bead clusters.

7 Thread the remaining three felt beads on to the second length of cord and stitch them into place, leaving 1cm (³/₈in) gaps between beads.

8 Create seed bead clusters about 1cm (³/₈in) from the felt beads.

9 Knot the second cord into place, just above the top cluster of beads on the first cord.

10 Decorate the knot and cut ends of cord with clusters of seed beads to finish.

Black Jack Bonanza

Change the colour scheme to black and purple, and worn with your 'little black dress' this necklace would send shivers down any pirate's spine!

Blackberry Glasses

Materials:

4 x purple felt pieces, 2.5 x 3cm (1 x 1¼in)

4 x black felt pieces, 1 x 9cm (½ x 3½in)

Selection of iridescent purple seed beads

Selection of iridescent purple bugle beads

Mauve embroidery thread

Medium cotton cord

Beading thread

2 x spectacle ends

Tools:

Scissors

Beading needle

Needle

Instructions:

1 Bind the felt pieces into four beads using embroidery thread and attach seed beads, following method F.

2 About 20cm (7¾in) from one end of the cord, stitch ten seed beads directly on to the cord to form a cluster.

3 Thread one felt bead on to the cord and position it about 2cm (¾in) away from the cluster.

4 Secure this bead by stab stitching directly into the cord using beading thread.

5 Stitch a second cluster and attach a second felt bead in the same way, again leaving about 2cm (¾in) between each.

6 Thread the cord through a spectacle end and double back on itself, securing the loop with another seed bead cluster.

7 Make sure the cord is cut to a comfortable length for the wearer. Repeat this beading pattern at the other end of the cord.

Bubble Gum

Although spectacle cords may have a reputation for being a little old-fashioned, nothing could be further from the truth with this bubbly, bright pink and blue colour scheme.

Prickly Pear Drops

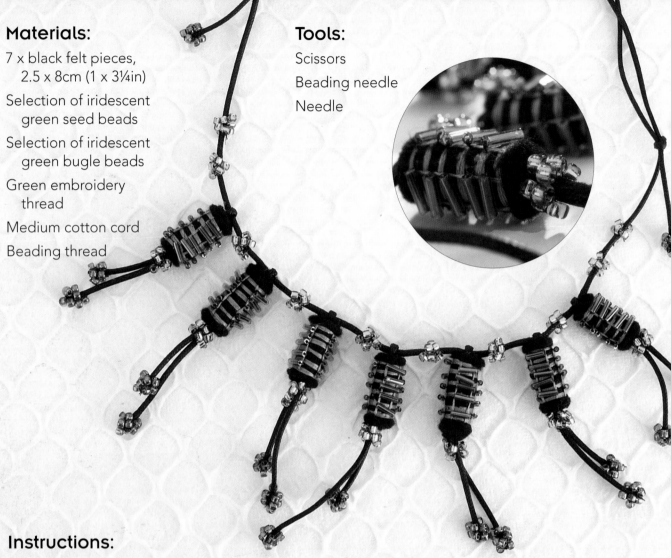

Materials:

7 x black felt pieces,
2.5 x 8cm (1 x 3¼in)

Selection of iridescent
green seed beads

Selection of iridescent
green bugle beads

Green embroidery
thread

Medium cotton cord

Beading thread

Tools:

Scissors

Beading needle

Needle

Instructions:

1 Bind the felt pieces into seven beads using embroidery thread and attach seed beads and bugle beads, following method D.

2 Cut seven lengths of cord, each about 14cm (5½in) long.

3 Fold one piece of cord in half, and pass the folded end through a felt bead. You will then have a loop at one end of the bead and the two cut ends of cord at the other.

4 Repeat for the other six felt beads.

5 Thread the loops on to cotton cord and space them out evenly, leaving gaps of about 3cm (1¼in) between each bead.

6 Secure these beads into place by stab stitching directly into the cord using beading thread. Make sure the beads are pushed firmly up to the cord at the top.

7 Stitch seed beads directly on to the cord to form a cluster at the base of each felt bead. Use ten seed beads for each cluster. Make sure the thread passes securely through both cords.

8 Stitch a cluster of seed beads on to each cut end of the cord.

9 Stitch a cluster of seed beads between each felt bead, again stitching directly into the cord.

10 Tie a sliding knot, and decorate the cut ends with further clusters of seed beads.

Tiger Lily

You will certainly get yourself noticed in this exotic and hot creation.
Simply change the colours to reds and oranges but keep the vivid impact
of the black cord. Sensational!

Rainbow Wristband

Materials:

15 x black felt pieces, 3 x 8cm (1¼ x 3¼in)
Selection of mixed rainbow seed beads
Black embroidery thread
Beading thread
100cm (39½in) length of round elastic

Tools:

Scissors
Beading needle
Needle

Instructions:

1 Bind the felt pieces into fifteen beads using embroidery thread and attach seed beads, following method C.

2 Thread one felt bead on to the elastic and move the bead to the centre.

3 Take the next felt bead and pass one end of the elastic through it from left to right. The other end of the elastic goes through the same bead, but from right to left.

4 Pull it gently into place alongside the first bead.

5 Repeat with all fifteen beads.

6 Finally, pass one end of the elastic back through the first bead, and tie the ends securely.

7 Gently pull the elastic round until the knot is hidden inside a felt bead.

Orange Drops

*Changing the colour scheme to oranges and pinks gives a light
and frivolous look to this easy-to-wear wristband.*

Violet Headband

Materials:

5 x white felt pieces, 8 x 11cm (3¼ x 4¼in)
Selection of silver/clear seed beads
Selection of pale purple seed beads
Selection of pale purple bugle beads
Silver sparkly embroidery thread
Beading thread
Medium cotton cord
Round elastic

Tools:

Scissors
Beading needle
Needle

Instructions:

1 Bind the felt pieces into five long beads using embroidery thread and attach seed beads and bugle beads, following method E.

2 Thread the felt beads on to the cord.

3 Keeping the beads in a straight line, use embroidery thread to darn the ends of the felt beads together using stab stitches.

4 Stitch bugle beads over the join to decorate.

5 Tie one end of the cord to the elastic and pull the knot up at least 4cm (1½in) inside the felt bead.

6 Trim the other end of the cord so that about 4cm (1½in) is protruding from the bead. Cut the elastic to length, making sure the overall length of the headband is correct, and tie the elastic on to the loose end of the cord.

7 Reposition the cord and elastic, so that both knots are hidden inside beads.

8 Bind the open ends of the felt beads with blanket stitch.

9 Add strings of seed beads, twisting and turning them around the felt beads and anchoring every now and then by stitching directly through the cord.

Aniseed Twist

This headband makes the perfect adornment for a bridesmaid. Match the colour to your wedding, and she will have not only a unique and beautiful piece of jewellery but also a treasured keepsake.

Fizzy Cherry Jellyfish

Materials:

1 x red felt piece, 3 x 6cm
  (1¼ x 2¼in)
Selection of pink seed beads
Selection of small silver beads
2 x red glass spacer beads
4 x medium silver beads
Pink embroidery thread
Beading thread
2 x silver calottes
1 x silver headpin
1 x silver bolt ring and eye

Tools:

Scissors
Flat-nose pliers
Round-nose pliers
Beading needle
Needle

Instructions:

1 Bind the felt piece into a bead using embroidery thread
and attach seed beads, following method H.

2 Using beading thread and seed beads, create a tassel-like
frond from the felt bead – thread the desired number of seed
beads on to the thread, then thread on a small silver bead.
Pass the needle back up through the seed beads (missing out
the silver bead) and anchor securely into the felt bead.

3 Repeat step 2 to create more fronds.

4 Thread one medium silver bead, the felt bead and a
second medium silver bead on to the headpin.

5 Form a loop in the end of the headpin.

6 Using beading thread, make a string of seed beads,
adding the medium silver beads, the glass spacer beads
and the felt bead to the centre of the string.

7 Pass the thread back through all the beads, rethreading right
the way round the necklace (so doubling its strength). Tie the
ends securely.

8 Attach a calotte around the seed bead at each end of the string.

9 Attach a bolt ring and eye to finish the fastening.

Fizzy Apple Jellyfish

Changing the colour of this necklace from cherry red and silver to green and gold gives this design a more mature, natural organic look.

Hazelnut Whirl Necklace

Materials:

3 x brown felt pieces, 2.5 x 6cm (1 x 2¼in)

42 x black spacer beads

4 x decorative glass beads

Selection of brown seed beads

Brown embroidery thread

Beading thread

1 x magnetic clasp

Tools:

Scissors

Beading needle

Needle

Instructions:

1 Bind the felt pieces into three beads using embroidery thread and attach seed beads, following method H.

2 Knot beading thread on to the magnetic clasp and thread seventeen spacer beads on to the thread.

3 Continue threading a combination of glass beads, spacer beads and felt beads to your chosen design. (Your design will depend on the exact beads you have sourced.)

4 Finish by threading the remaining seventeen spacer beads on to the thread.

5 Pass the thread back through the magnetic clasp and rethread it right the way round the necklace (so doubling its strength). Tie the ends securely and hide the knots inside the beads.

Ice Cube Whirl

Transform this necklace from warm, nutty brown into cool, crisp elegance simply by changing the colour to ice cool blues. Irregular-shaped glass beads complement the structure of the seed bead spirals.

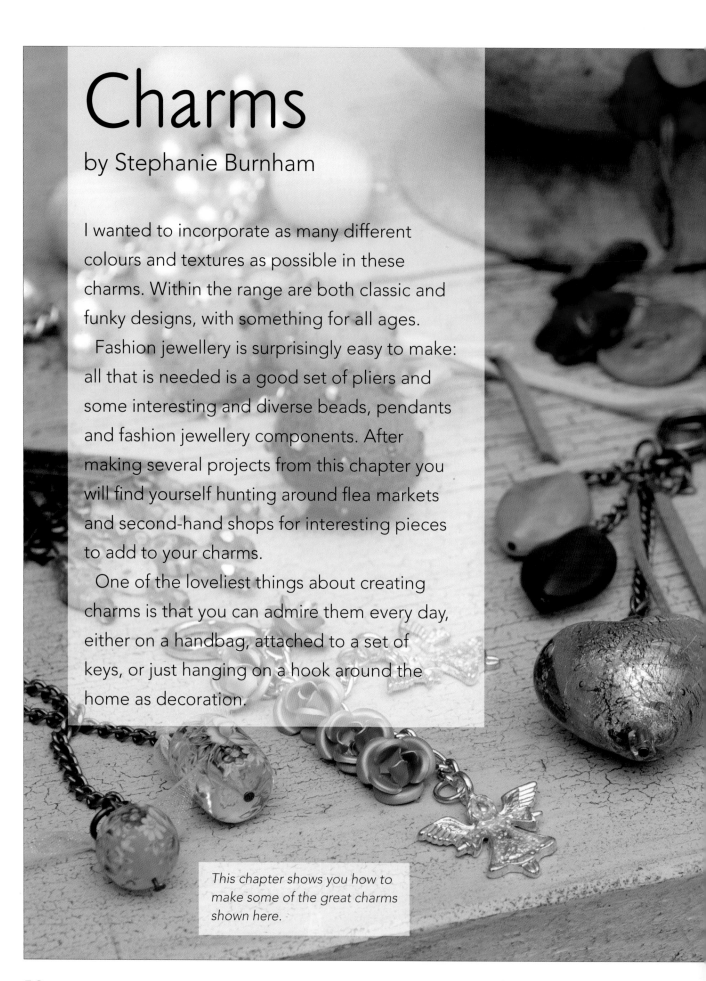

Charms

by Stephanie Burnham

I wanted to incorporate as many different colours and textures as possible in these charms. Within the range are both classic and funky designs, with something for all ages.

Fashion jewellery is surprisingly easy to make: all that is needed is a good set of pliers and some interesting and diverse beads, pendants and fashion jewellery components. After making several projects from this chapter you will find yourself hunting around flea markets and second-hand shops for interesting pieces to add to your charms.

One of the loveliest things about creating charms is that you can admire them every day, either on a handbag, attached to a set of keys, or just hanging on a hook around the home as decoration.

This chapter shows you how to make some of the great charms shown here.

Heart Happening

Materials:

1 x glass heart bead
2 x glass beads
Suede ribbon
Medium craft chain
8 x jump rings
5 x pink seed beads
2 x flat leather crimps
3 x headpins
1 x keyring fob

Tools:

Cutting pliers
Round-nosed pliers
Flat-nosed pliers
Scissors

Instructions:

1 Wire the three glass beads with headpins, creating a loop at the top of each bead and adding a pink seed bead at either end of the rectangular glass bead and one pink seed bead below and one above the heart bead.

2 Attach three differing lengths of chain to the keyring fob using jump rings. Attach the three glass beads to the bottom of the three lengths of chain, again using jump rings.

3 Cut two lengths of suede ribbon and attach a flat leather crimp to one end of each using flat-nosed pliers.

4 Using jump rings, attach the suede ribbons to the keyring fob. You can then cut the bottom end of the ribbon at an angle to give a neat finish.

Spring Heart

A copper-coloured chain, clasp and jump rings are used to set off green beads and suede ribbons, creating a lush, spring-like feel to this charm.

Pastel Pearls

Materials:

Selection of faux
pearl beads

4 x large wrapped beads

4 x 4mm fire-polished
crystals

Medium copper-coloured
craft chain

14 x headpins

1 x copper-coloured
jump ring

1 x large copper-coloured
lobster clasp

Tools:

Cutting pliers

Round-nosed pliers

Instructions:

1 Wire a selection of pearl
beads on to headpins,
creating a loop at the top of
each set of beads.

2 Do the same with the
four wrapped beads using a
4mm fire-polished crystal at
the base of each bead.

3 Cut a section of chain
to the required length and
attach it to the large lobster
clasp using the jump ring.

4 Finally, carefully open
up each loop at the top
of each set of beads and
attach to the chain one
by one.

Pretty in Pearls

A silver-coloured chain is teamed with beads in cool blue and pink to make a sumptuous but subtle charm that looks great attached to a purse.

Eastern Flowers

Materials:

1 x large accent bead

2 x medium accent beads

Suede ribbon

Organza ribbon

Medium silver-coloured craft chain

8 x silver-coloured jump rings

3 x headpins

2 x silver-coloured flat leather crimps

1 x large silver-coloured lobster clasp

Tools:

Cutting pliers

Round-nosed pliers

Flat-nosed pliers

Scissors

Instructions:

1 Using headpins, wire the three accent beads, creating a loop at the top of each bead.

2 Attach three varying lengths of chain to the large lobster clasp with jump rings.

3 Attach the three glass beads to the bottom ends of the chain, again with jump rings.

4 Cut two lengths of suede ribbon and attach a flat leather crimp to one end of each using flat-nosed pliers.

5 Attach the two lengths of suede to the large lobster clasp with jump rings. The bottom ends of the suede can then be cut at an angle to give a nice finish.

6 Finally, cut three pieces of ribbon about 5cm (2in) long, thread a ribbon through each jump ring attaching an accent bead and tie a double knot. The ribbon can then be cut off at an angle to the required length.

Oriental Garden

These flower-painted accent beads give an oriental feel to a charm. Instead of the blue, try a pink and green theme. The little wisps of organza ribbon make the prettiest finishing touch.

Fairytale Butterfly

Materials:

Selection of faux pearls
1 x large butterfly charm
Medium copper-coloured craft chain
10 x copper-coloured jump rings
9 x headpins
1 x large copper-coloured lobster clasp

Tools:

Cutting pliers
Round-nosed pliers

Instructions:

1 Wire a selection of pearl beads on to headpins, creating a loop at the top of each set of beads.

2 Cut a piece of chain the required length and attach it to the large lobster clasp using a jump ring.

3 Using round-nosed pliers, open up a jump ring, slip a wired pearl bead on to it, then slip the jump ring on to the central chain and close it.

4 Continue adding pearls in the same manner until the charm is complete.

5 Attach the butterfly charm to the end of the chain using a jump ring.

Pearly Butterfly

Change from the warm, gold and bronze tones of the charm opposite to make this pretty variation using pastel-coloured pearls with silver and a more delicate butterfly.

Gardener's Delight

Materials:

5 x themed charms

Medium gold-coloured craft chain

8 x gold-coloured jump rings

1 x large gold-coloured lobster clasp

Tools:

Cutting pliers

Round-nosed pliers

Instructions:

1 Cut three pieces of chain of varying lengths.

2 Attach all three lengths to the lobster clasp with jump rings.

3 Using a jump ring, attach a charm to the base of all three chain lengths.

4 Add the last two charms to the two longer lengths of chain about one-third of the way up the chain lengths.

Summer Fun

Beaded flip-flops complete this sizzling charm, which would make a lovely gift for someone with a summer birthday.

Hippy Chick

Materials:

9 x mother of pearl
    dyed shapes

11 x gold-coloured
    jump rings

2 x headpins

2 x feature beads

4 x seed beads

1 x large gold-coloured
    lobster clasp

Tools:

Cutting pliers

Round-nosed pliers

Instructions:

1 Take a single jump ring,
open it up using round-
nosed pliers, thread on a
round and a square shape
and close the jump ring.

2 Repeat until you have
four shapes joined together.

3 Make a second chain link,
this time with five shapes.

4 Attach the chain with five
links to the large lobster
clasp, then attach the chain
with four shapes to the
jump ring of the chain with
five links.

5 Wire the two feature
beads on to headpins,
placing a seed bead at the
top and bottom of each
larger bead.

6 Attach each bead to the
bottom end of a chain link
using a jump ring.

Pretty in Pink

This version of the charm looks great with jeans, and the luscious feature beads add a touch of class.

Bubble Gum

Materials:
3 x large beaded beads
6 x small faux pearls
2 x medium faux pearls
Large silver-coloured craft chain
6 x headpins
9 x silver-coloured jump rings
1 x silver-coloured keyring fob

Tools:
Cutting pliers
Round-nosed pliers

Instructions:

1 Wire the large beaded beads on to headpins, placing a small pearl bead at the top and bottom of each bead, and creating a loop at the top of each set of beads. Here, the smaller beaded bead did not need a pearl at the top; just use your own judgment when choosing beads.

2 Cut three pieces of craft chain of varying lengths and attach them to the keyring fob with jump rings.

3 Attach the three beaded beads to the base of each chain using jump rings, placing the largest bead on to the longest length of chain.

4 Wire the remaining pearls on to headpins and attach them to the chain as you wish.

Red-Hot

*This red and gold version of the charm makes a
really dazzling decoration for a plain bag.*

Celebration Hearts

Materials:

1 x large shell heart

2 x silver-coloured hearts

3 x glass feature beads

Large silver-coloured craft chain

3 x headpins

9 x jump rings

1 x keyring fob

Tools:

Cutting pliers

Round-nosed pliers

Instructions:

1 Wire all three feature beads with headpins, creating a loop at the top of each bead.

2 Cut three varying lengths of chain and attach to the keyring fob with jump rings.

3 Attach the large heart to the longest length of chain, and the two slightly smaller hearts to the other two chain ends, all with jump rings.

4 Finally position all three feature beads onto the chain lengths with jump rings.

Hearts and Gold

Glitzy gold and cream-coloured hearts make this charm the perfect accessory for a leather bag.

Traveller's Tale

Materials:

2 x large copper-coloured beads

3 x medium copper-coloured beads

10 x heart-shaped copper-coloured spacer beads

5 x headpins

Large copper-coloured craft chain

6 x jump rings

1 x large copper-coloured lobster clasp

Tools:

Cutting pliers

Round-nosed pliers

Instructions:

1 Cut three pieces of craft chain of varying lengths and attach them to the large lobster clasp using one large jump ring.

2 Wire up the two large and three medium metal beads, placing one spacer bead at the top and bottom of each.

3 Attach the two larger and one medium wired-up beads to the base of each chain length.

4 Attach one of the two remaining medium beads directly to the lobster clasp with a jump ring.

5 Attach the second half-way up the longest length of chain, again using a jump ring.

Silver Charmer

This charm looks great against dark clothes or bags, and could even be used to brighten a dark corner of your house.

Venetian Splendour

Materials:

2 x large glass feature beads

3 x medium glass feature beads

1 x 8mm bicone crystal

6 x headpins

1 x large silver-coloured lobster clasp

Tools:

Cutting pliers

Round-nosed pliers

Instructions:

1 Cut the head from a headpin, thread the piece of wire through one of the glass feature beads and create a loop at each end of the bead.

2 Repeat in the same manner until all five beads have two loops each.

3 Take one of the large beads, carefully open up one of the loops and slip the lobster clasp on to the loop. Close the loop again.

4 Open the loop at the other end and slip on the second big bead, closing the loop afterwards.

5 Repeat until all five beads are joined together using the links that have been created.

6 To finish, wire the crystal bead up and fix to the loop of the last feature bead added.

Amber Elegance

This alternative version of the charm replaces cool pink with amber tones to create a precious-looking golden glow.

First Love

Materials:
1 x glass heart feature bead

5 x faux pearls

1 x medium silver-coloured craft chain

1 x jump ring

4 x headpins

1 x large silver-coloured lobster clasp

Tools:
Cutting pliers

Round-nosed pliers

Instructions:

1 Remove the head from a headpin, then thread on one pearl, a glass heart and a pearl.

2 Using round-nosed pliers, create a loop at each end of the beads.

3 Wire up two other pearls using headpins and make loops at both ends of these two beads.

4 Cut four sections of chain containing only two links per section.

5 Using a jump ring, attach the first two links to the lobster clasp, then open up one of the loops on the single pearls and thread it through the second link from the clasp. Close it again with round-nosed pliers.

6 Continue to open and close links as you work towards the base of the charm.

7 To finish, wire the final pearl onto a headpin and attach to the last link of the chain.

Golden Heart
This sumptuous golden version of the charm makes a beautiful gift for a loved one.

Posh Pom-Poms

Materials:

3 x large beaded felt balls
Medium gold-coloured craft chain
1 x jump ring
3 x headpins
1 x gold-coloured keyring fob
Suede ribbon in two colours
4 x flower sequins

Tools:

Cutting pliers
Round-nosed pliers
Scissors

Instructions:

1 Take two of the felt balls and wire them on to headpins, adding a flower sequin at each end. Create a loop at the top of each bead.

2 Cut two 15cm (6in) lengths of suede ribbon. Place the two pieces together and thread them through the loop on the keyring fob. Tie the lengths together using a single knot underneath the fixing point of the keyring fob.

3 Take the third felt ball and thread it on to one of the lengths of suede. Cut the suede to the length you require then make a knot below the felt ball to secure it.

4 Trim the remaining lengths of suede to the desired length, cutting at an angle for a neat finish.

5 Cut a length of chain, attach it to the keyring fob with a jump ring, and then attach the two wired beads to the chain as desired.

Moody Blues

Blue and purple felt balls teamed with silver add a
touch of subtlety to a chunky charm.

Necklaces

by Stephanie Burnham

I love fashion necklaces, so to be asked to create a complete set of designs was a delight.

The brief is fashionable, stylish and funky necklaces with a great infusion of colour, as strong colours are all around us at the moment in fashion, home furnishing and jewellery.

All the designs are very easy to complete. Let your imagination run wild: don't be afraid to adapt or develop the original designs, allowing your creativity to flow.

Big is beautiful in fashion jewellery so why not make a statement? If this is not quite you, use smaller beads to adapt the designs and make something to suit your taste.

The examples shown here represent the type of necklaces that this chapter will enable you to make.

Dragonfly Ball

Materials:

100cm (39½in)
  craft chain

6 x dragonfly charms

1 x large toggle clasp

8 x jump rings

Tools:

Cutting pliers

Round-nosed pliers

Instructions:

1 Measure and cut a length of chain so that it fits around the neck of the wearer and in addition to this, has a drop section long enough to hang the charms from.

2 Attach the loop part of the toggle to one end of the chain using a jump ring.

3 Using a jump ring, attach the T-bar end to the chain where you wish the chain to join at the front of the neck, allowing the section of chain at the end to fall down towards the chest.

4 Attach the charms using jump rings, starting at the base of the drop and working upwards so that the charms just about touch each other, thus avoiding any gaps in the design. Attach four to the drop and two to the section that goes round the neck.

84

Silver Hearts

Hearts in various sizes replace the dragonflies in this sumptuous silver version of the necklace.

Graceful Glass

Materials:

1 x glass pendant

50cm (19¾in) faux suede ribbon in two colours

2 x flat leather crimps

2 x jump rings

1 x lobster clasp

Tools:

Flat-nosed pliers

Scissors

Instructions:

1 Cut both pieces of suede ribbon to the required necklace length.

2 Pass both pieces through the loop on the pendant.

3 Fix the flat leather crimps to both ends of the necklace.

4 Attach a jump ring to one side of the necklace and a jump ring and the lobster clasp to the other.

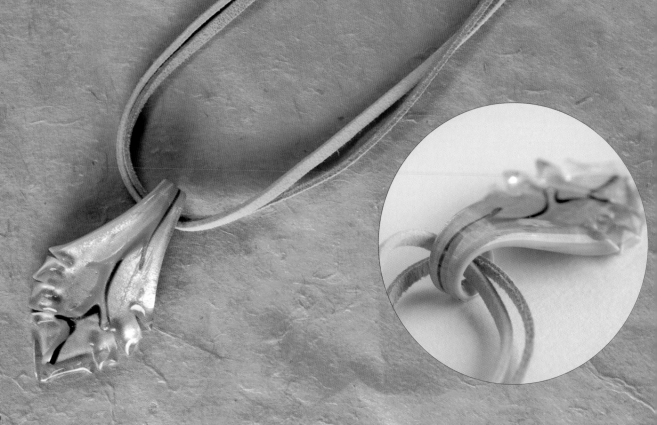

Gold Leaf

This striking pendant looks great teamed up with warm beige and bright turquoise suede.

Linen Lariat

Materials:

200cm (79in) stringing cord

6 x wrapped beads

12 x faux pearls

Tools:

Collapsible eye needle

Scissors

Instructions:

1 Make a knot in the stringing cord within 10cm (4in) of the tail end.

2 Thread on one pearl, one wrapped and one pearl bead. Make a second knot directly after the last pearl added.

3 Leaving an 11cm (4³/₈in) gap, make another knot, thread on a further pearl, a wrapped and a pearl bead and make a second knot directly after the last pearl added.

4 Continue in the same way until all the beads are added.

5 To finish, knot the two ends together to secure.

Creamy Blue Lariat

These pale blue pearls and creamy linen beads create a cool look for summer.

Precious Stone

Materials:

Pendant with central hole
2 x medium metal beads
100cm (39½in) suede ribbon
2 x flat leather crimps
4 x crimp beads
Lobster clasp

Tools:

Round-nosed pliers
Flat-nosed pliers
Scissors

Instructions:

1 Place the two ends of suede together and pass the loop through the central hole of the pendant. Pass the two ends of suede through the loop and pull up, securing the suede on to the pendant.

2 Thread on a crimp bead at the base of each length of suede just above the pendant. Secure them using flat-nosed pliers.

3 Thread a metal bead on to each length of suede and add another crimp bead above each bead.

4 Finish by attaching the flat leather crimps and lobster clasp after sizing the necklace to fit.

Polished Heart

This natural-looking necklace has knots instead of crimp beads around the copper-coloured beads.

Caribbean Colours

Materials:

A selection of large fashion beads
A selection of copper beads
Tiger tail wire
2 x calottes
2 x jump rings
1 x lobster clasp

Tools:

Cutting pliers
Round-nosed pliers

Instructions:

1 Lay the beads out either on a design board or a soft cloth and have a play at different variations and combinations of beads and colours.

2 When you are happy with the design, cut a length of tiger tail to the required length of necklace, allowing an extra 15cm (6in) each end for finishing.

3 Thread the beads on to the tiger tail in the required order.

4 Finish by adding the calottes, jump rings and lobster clasp in the usual manner.

Cool and Chunky
This shorter version of the necklace in turquoise and silver is a stunning alternative.

93

Glam Rocks

Materials:

100cm (39½in) copper-coloured chain

7 x decorated feature beads

2 x jump rings

Lobster clasp

Tools:

Round-nosed pliers

Cutting pliers

Instructions:

1 Cut a section of copper chain to the required length of the necklace.

2 Thread on the seven large decorated beads.

3 Add the jump rings and lobster clasp to the ends of the chain.

Spring Fever

These vibrant green beads make a striking necklace with a spring-like feel.

Caged Copper

Materials:

100cm (39½in) wire mesh ribbon

A selection of copper beads

Large embellished bead

2 x flat leather crimps

2 x jump rings

Lobster clasp

Tools:

Flat-nosed pliers

Scissors

Instructions:

1 Thread the large embellished bead down to the centre point of the wire mesh ribbon and tie a double knot at each side of the bead to secure it.

2 Open up one end of the wire tube and slide a bead down until it sits next to the embellished bead. Tie a knot directly after the bead to close the wire mesh once again.

3 Next, pass a metal bead down over the mesh and tie a knot directly after it to secure it.

4 Continue to alternate in the same manner on either side of the large embellished bead until the necklace has reached the desired length.

5 Add the flat leather crimps, jump rings and lobster clasp to the ends to finish.

Note: Bear in mind, when planning your design, that knotting shortens the ribbon quite a bit.

Marvellous Mesh

Wire mesh ribbon is a fun and versatile material. In this pink and silver version of the necklace, some of it has been left beadless for a different effect.

Beach Lariat

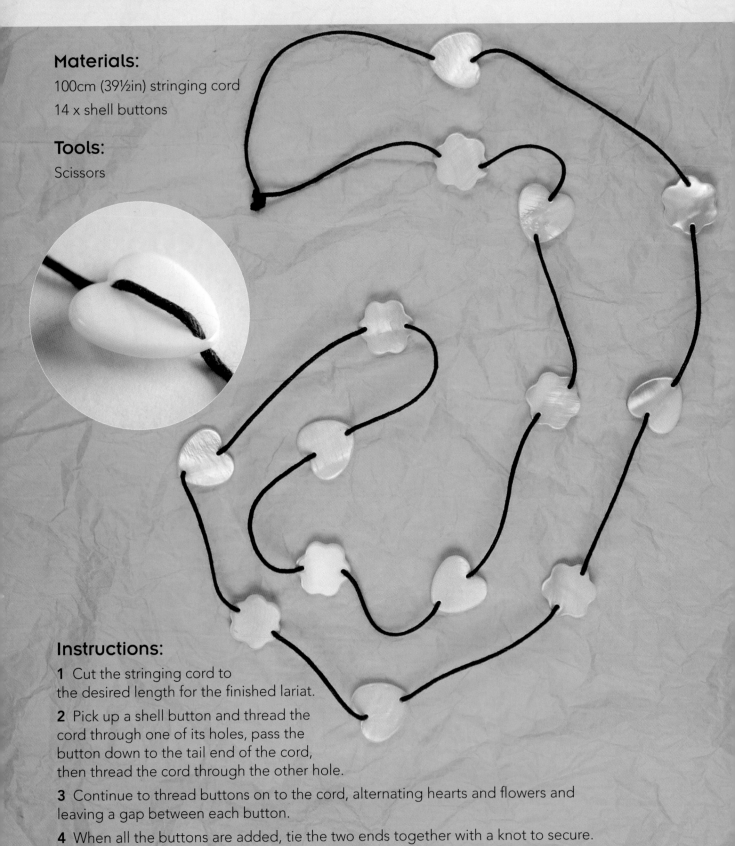

Materials:

100cm (39½in) stringing cord
14 x shell buttons

Tools:

Scissors

Instructions:

1 Cut the stringing cord to
the desired length for the finished lariat.

2 Pick up a shell button and thread the
cord through one of its holes, pass the
button down to the tail end of the cord,
then thread the cord through the other hole.

3 Continue to thread buttons on to the cord, alternating hearts and flowers and
leaving a gap between each button.

4 When all the buttons are added, tie the two ends together with a knot to secure.

Hearts and Flowers

Green cord and yellow buttons give this longer lariat a natural, spring-like feel.
You need 200cm (79in) of cord and twenty shell buttons for this version.

Organza Garland

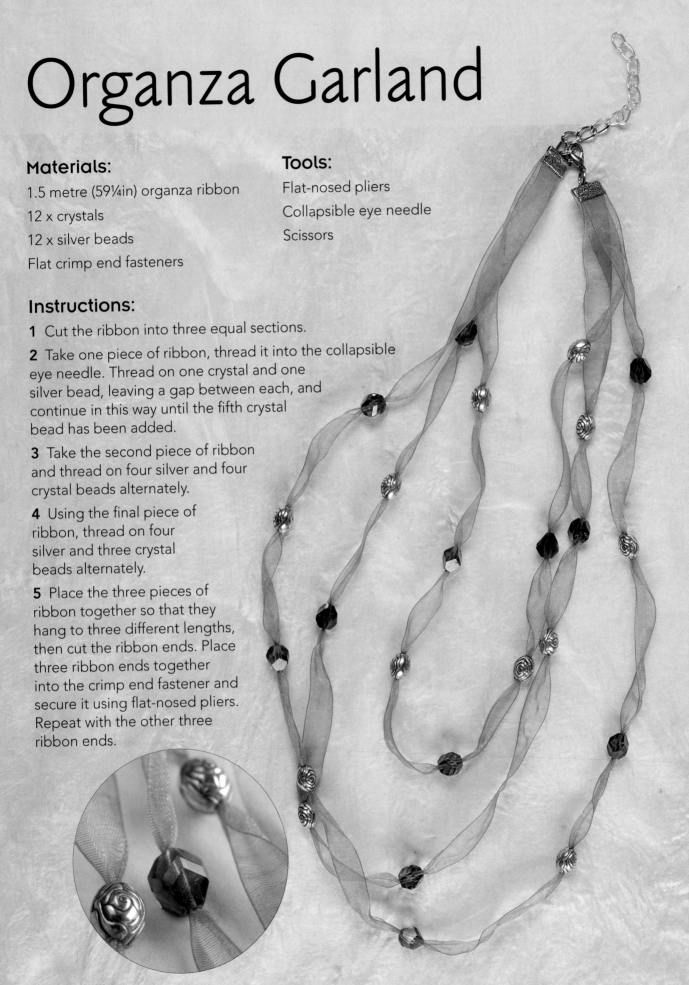

Materials:
1.5 metre (59¼in) organza ribbon
12 x crystals
12 x silver beads
Flat crimp end fasteners

Tools:
Flat-nosed pliers
Collapsible eye needle
Scissors

Instructions:

1 Cut the ribbon into three equal sections.

2 Take one piece of ribbon, thread it into the collapsible eye needle. Thread on one crystal and one silver bead, leaving a gap between each, and continue in this way until the fifth crystal bead has been added.

3 Take the second piece of ribbon and thread on four silver and four crystal beads alternately.

4 Using the final piece of ribbon, thread on four silver and three crystal beads alternately.

5 Place the three pieces of ribbon together so that they hang to three different lengths, then cut the ribbon ends. Place three ribbon ends together into the crimp end fastener and secure it using flat-nosed pliers. Repeat with the other three ribbon ends.

Ruby Crystals

Ruby-coloured crystals and the palest of pink organza ribbon make a beautiful necklace with a delicate and decadent style.

Faux Pearl Fancy

Materials:

100cm (39½in) craft chain

31 faux pearls in various colours and sizes

31 x headpins

3 x jump rings

Lobster clasp

Tools:

Cutting pliers

Round-nosed pliers

Instructions:

1 Cut two lengths of chain, the first to come from the nape of the neck around to the front and the second to come from the nape of the neck around to the front, then to dangle down forming a 'Y' shape.

2 Create the 'Y' by linking the two chains together with a jump ring.

3 Size the necklace to fit. Remember you can cut excess length away at this point. Attach the lobster clasp to the ends of the chain using jump rings.

4 Wire the selection of faux pearls with headpins, creating a loop at the top of each pearl.

5 Before you start to add the pearls, check the length of the chain at the front, as it may need shortening.

6 Starting at the base, add pearls, continuing up the chain to finish.

Copper Tones

Copper, bronze and gold-coloured faux pearls look amazing with these deep-coloured crystals, making a necklace with a fiery feel.

Roman Amulet

Materials:

Memory wire choker
10g size 8 seed beads
Pendant
2 metal feature beads

Tools:

Flat-nosed pliers

Instructions:

1 Using flat-nosed pliers, bend one end of the memory wire over to form a loop. This stops the beads from falling off the end.

2 Thread on the seed beads until you have not quite reached the centre of the choker.

3 Thread on the metal bead, then the pendant.

4 Repeat the bead sequence on the other side, leaving about 1cm (³/₈in) at the end for making the loop.

5 Once the beads are in position, bend the end into a loop to secure.

Cherry Red

This version of the choker uses bright red size 6 seed beads and four silver-coloured feature beads, which perfectly complement the gorgeous pendant.

Petals Pendant

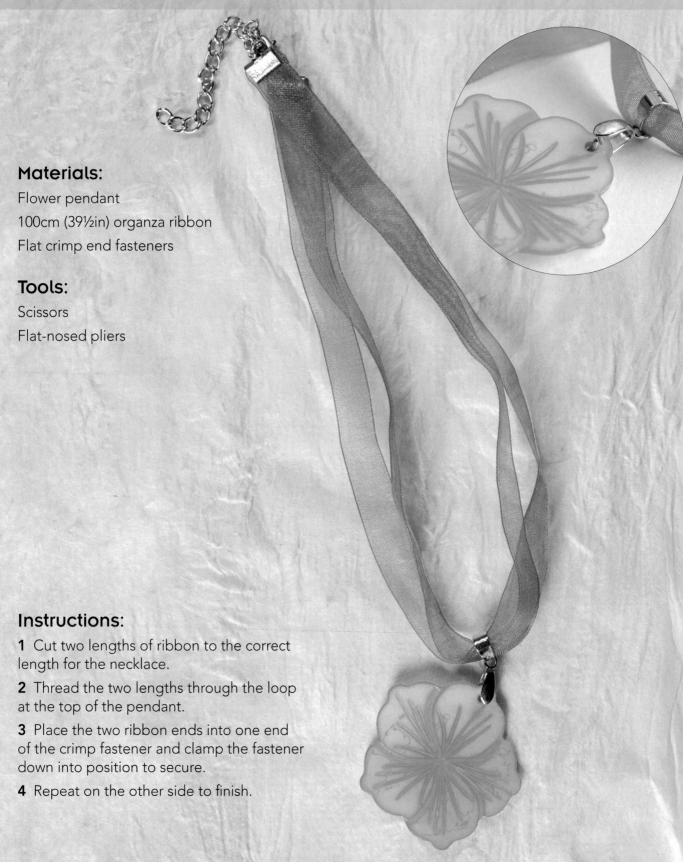

Materials:

Flower pendant

100cm (39½in) organza ribbon

Flat crimp end fasteners

Tools:

Scissors

Flat-nosed pliers

Instructions:

1 Cut two lengths of ribbon to the correct length for the necklace.

2 Thread the two lengths through the loop at the top of the pendant.

3 Place the two ribbon ends into one end of the crimp fastener and clamp the fastener down into position to secure.

4 Repeat on the other side to finish.

Go Green

This pendant has a luscious look and when teamed up with the cool green ribbon it creates a pretty and sophisticated necklace.

Leaves and Sparkle

Tiara

Materials:

Silver-lined crystal Delica beads
Silver-plated tiara band
0.4mm silver-plated wire

Tools:

Round-nosed pliers
Flat-nosed pliers
Side-cutter pliers
Jeweller's ring clamp (optional)

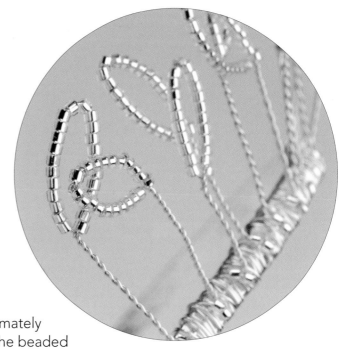

Instructions:

1 Cut a 60cm (23½in) length of wire, thread approximately twenty beads into the centre of the wire and bend the beaded section round into a small leaf shape.

2 Hold the beaded leaf shape between your fingers or in a ring clamp and clasp the two strands of wire about 2cm (¾in) away from the bead in the round-nosed pliers. Hold the pliers still and twist the leaf shape until the two lengths of wire are twisted tightly together.

3 Bend the excess wires outwards and continue adding beads in the same way until you have created a row of approximately fifteen twisted stems 1cm (³/₈in) apart, leaving at least 5cm (2in) of wire at each end. Make the outer strands slightly shorter so that the tiara is highest at the front and tapers down each side.

4 Starting from the centre of the tiara band, attach the strands by wrapping the excess wire tightly around it, using the flat-nosed pliers to flatten the wire to the band.

5 Decorate the front of the tiara band by wrapping an 80cm (31½in) length of wire around the band, threading beads on to the wire as you pass it between the strands. Secure it by wrapping the excess wire around the band several times at each end.

6 Gently bend each leaf to complete the design.

Hairpin

This simple design lends itself well to this gold-plated wire hairpin. Several could be worn together to create a stunning effect.

Bramble

Tiara

Materials:

70 amethyst and rose quartz stone
   chip beads
Silver-plated tiara band
0.4mm silver-plated wire

Tools:

Round-nosed pliers
Flat-nosed pliers
Side-cutter pliers
Jeweller's ring clamp (optional)

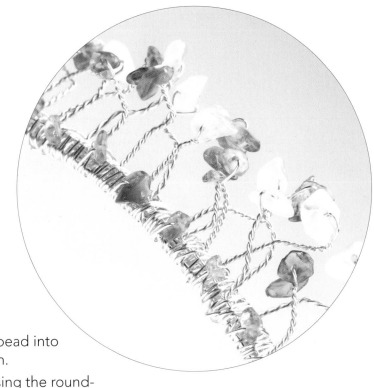

Instructions:

1 Cut a 60cm (23½in) length of wire, thread a bead into
the centre of the wire and bend the ends down.

2 Hold the bead between your fingers and, using the round-
nosed pliers, hold the two strands of wire about 1.5cm (¾in)
away from the bead. Hold the pliers still and twist the bead until
the two lengths of wire are twisted tightly together.

3 Bend the excess wires outwards and continue adding beads
in the same way until you have created a row of approximately
thirty-eight twisted stems of various lengths, about 5mm (¼in)
apart, leaving at least 5cm (2in) of wire at each end. Make the
outer strands slightly shorter so that the tiara is highest at the
front and tapers down each side.

4 Starting from the centre of the tiara band, attach the strands
by wrapping the excess wire tightly around it. Use the flat-nosed
pliers to flatten the wire to the band.

5 Decorate the front of the tiara band by wrapping an 80cm
(31½in) length of wire around it, threading beads on to the wire
as you pass it between the strands. Secure it by wrapping the
excess wire around the band several times at each end.

6 Finally, bend each strand using flat-nosed pliers to create
the messy bramble effect.

Hairpin

These lovely, creamy green amazonite stone chips give an
interesting and earthy look to this hairpin.

Flower Garden

Tiara

Materials:

35 x 3mm faux pearls

9 x 5mm faux pearls

39 x 4mm crystal beads

Silver-plated tiara band

0.4mm silver-plated wire

Tools:

Round-nosed pliers

Flat-nosed pliers

Side-cutter pliers

Jeweller's ring clamp (optional)

Instructions:

1 Cut a 60cm (23½in) length of wire, thread five small pearls into the centre and bend the ends down. Wrap them into a circle to create a tiny, abstract flower.

2 Hold the beads between your fingers and use the round-nosed pliers to hold the two strands of wire about 3cm (1¼in) away from the bead. Hold the pliers still and twist the bead until the two lengths of wire are twisted tightly together.

3 Bend the excess wires outwards and continue in the same way until you have created a row consisting of eight flowers made of both pearls and crystals; nine strands topped with a single large pearl; and nineteen strands of various lengths, each with a single crystal at its tip. The strands should be approximately 5mm (¼in) apart, leaving at least 5cm (2in) of wire at each end.

4 Starting from the centre of the tiara band, attach the strands by wrapping the excess wire tightly around it. Use the flat-nosed pliers to flatten the wire to the band.

5 Decorate the front of the tiara band by wrapping an 80cm (31½in) length of wire around the band, threading small beads on to the wire as you pass it between the strands. Secure it by wrapping the excess wire around the band several times at each end.

6 Gently bend the strands in different directions to complete the design.

Hairpin

Use gold-plated wire and rich, red crystals teamed with pearls to complement a deep red dress or a bouquet of red roses.

Woodland

Tiara

Materials:

18 x 4mm clear crystal beads
24 x 4mm pink crystal beads
Silver-plated tiara bands
0.4mm silver-plated wire

Tools:

Round-nosed pliers
Flat-nosed pliers
Side-cutter pliers
Jeweller's ring clamp (optional)

Instructions:

1 Cut a 60cm (23½in) length of wire, thread a bead into the centre and bend the ends down.

2 Hold the bead between your fingers and hold the two strands of wire about 1cm (³/₈in) away from the bead using the round-nosed pliers. Hold the pliers still and twist the bead until the two lengths of wire are twisted tightly together.

3 Bend the excess wires outwards, add a bead to create another branch on each side and twist. Continue adding beads in the same way until you have created a row of six tree shapes and nine straight strands, approximately 1cm (³/₈in) apart, topped with a single pink bead. Leave at least 5cm (2in) of wire at each end.

4 Starting from the centre of the tiara band, attach the strands by wrapping the excess wire tightly around it. Use the flat-nosed pliers to flatten the wire to the band.

5 Decorate the front of the tiara band by wrapping an 80cm (31½in) length of wire around the band, threading beads on to the wire as you pass it between the strands. Secure it by wrapping the excess wire around the band several times at each end.

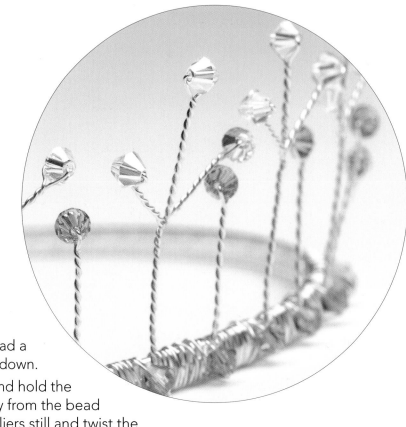

Hairpin

A wintery, antique look can be achieved by using brass-plated wire and clear crystals to create the hairpin.

Wild Women Art Brooches

by Sarah Lawrence

Making textile art brooches is a lovely way to express your creativity. All the projects here are open to your own interpretation and I sincerely hope that you have as much fun making pieces of art to wear as I do.

Very little needs to be purchased to make these fun brooches, and by asking friends and relatives all sorts of charms, threads and background materials can be acquired. Those things that need to be purchased are widely available through reputable retail stores and over the internet.

Note that some experience of free machine embroidery may be required for some of the projects in this chapter.

These wild textile art brooches are great fun to make using the instructions and techniques presented in this chapter.

Basic tools:

Felt

Scissors

Needles (including a beading needle)

Sewing and embroidery threads

Brooch backs

Templates and brooch backs

Each of the projects in this chapter uses one of the four templates shown here. Each of these templates has been reproduced at full size, ready to be used.

Finishing off the brooch

Apart from the instructions in the project, you may choose to hide any untidy thread ends on the back of the brooch by cutting out an extra medium weight template to match the body shape and colour. Place it on the back of the brooch, then depending on the design, either oversew the edges, or attach the back to the front with invisible or matching thread.

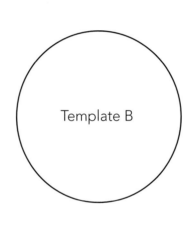

Template A

Template B

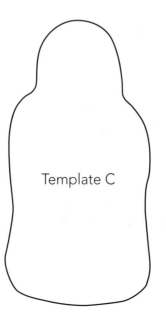

Template C

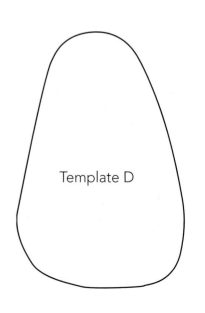

Template D

Once you have completed each Wild Woman art brooch, you will need to affix a brooch back to the finished piece. There are numerous different types, from brass backs that can be stitched on, to simple adhesive backs as shown above.

The positioning of the brooch back is very important: make sure you attach it within the top third of the piece, so that the piece hangs well when being worn. If you place the back too low down, the top can curl over.

Swaddling Sister

Instructions:

1 Using the blue felt-tipped pen, colour one side of the heavy interlining template. This makes any spaces between the beads less obvious.

2 Sew on the face charm with the needle and thread.

3 Outline the charm with a mix of all of the seed beads, then continue to fill in the rest of the body with beads. Stitch in groups of three beads as this allows gentle curves to be made. Leave a 2mm (1⁄16in) gap around the edge of the template.

4 Stitch feature beads on in a trailing line, using a seed bead on each to anchor them in place (see detail opposite).

5 Place the medium weight interlining on the back. Using groups of three to five seed beads, oversew the two edges until a rope-like effect is created all around the template.

6 Attach a brooch back to complete the piece.

Ruby!
Using a variety of flower-shaped feature beads and warmer colours changes the feel of the brooch dramatically.

Artemis Ascendent

Materials:

White cotton, approximately 15cm (6in) square

Black solvent-based permanent ink pad

A 15cm (6in) piece of black non-woven medium weight interlining

A 15cm (6in) piece of non-woven white heavy weight interlining

Pink and blue fabric paints

Small amount of wadding

Magenta (18009F) face stamp

Permanent black marker pen

Nine silver sequins

Nine seed beads

Tools:

Basic tool kit

Paintbrush

Pencil

Sewing machine

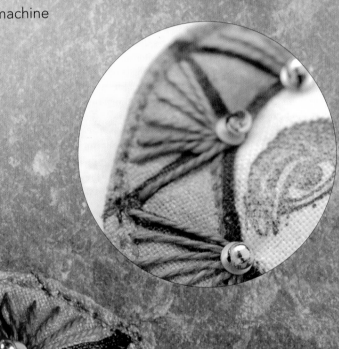

Instructions:

1 Use the face stamp to print a face on to the cotton with the permanent ink pad and allow to dry.

2 Draw template B around the printed motif with the pencil, then place the cotton on to the medium weight interlining.

3 Using the sewing machine, stitch around the outline of the face motif and the outer circle, then cut away the excess fabric.

4 Mark the triangles with the permanent black marker pen to plan out a pattern of triangles round the outer ring, then use the fabric paints to colour them. Make sure you paint over the outer stitch line as this will prevent fraying. Allow to dry.

5 Cut small slits in the interlining from the back and stuff the face and outer halo with wadding to give a gentle raised effect. Stitch the background closed.

6 Cut a piece of non-woven heavy interlining to cover the back, then use simple hand stitches and a few sequins and beads (see detail opposite) to secure the interlining and decorate the halo.

7 Stitch or glue a brooch back in position on the back to complete the brooch.

Diana Resplendent

An irregular border on the halo gives a pleasing varied effect to the finished piece and is very simple to do.

Daffy-Down-Dilly

Materials:

Artgirlz Heart and Face rubber stamps

Black and red solvent-based permanent ink pads

Template A cut from cotton

Template A cut from non-woven black heavy interlining

Template A cut from non-woven white medium weight interlining

A selection of orange and green seed beads

Eleven gold flower sequins

Heart and star feature beads

Tools:

Basic tool kit

Sewing machine

Instructions:

1 Print the face and heart stamps on to the cotton template using black and red ink pads respectively.

2 Attach the printed cotton template to the medium interlining template by carefully stitching around the outline of the face and heart with orange cotton thread.

3 Use free machine embroidery to fill the remaining space.

4 Attach the flower sequins around the face, securing each with a seed bead (see detail opposite), then attach beads all around the heart and face.

5 To create the fringe effect, take a needle up through the interlining and thread three orange seed beads, then a heart feature bead, then a single green seed bead on to the needle.

6 Miss the green bead out and pass the needle back through the feature bead and orange beads above. Take the needle back down through the interlining and secure to create the first part of the fringe.

7 Continue working along the fringe at the bottom and below the central heart shape, varying the number of seed beads and feature beads on each part as shown opposite.

8 Stitch the heavy interlining template on to the back, then glue or stitch a brooch back on to the piece to finish.

Polly Potter

Sometimes subtle changes in colour can make a difference, as shown in this variation.

Bonnie Wee Rosie

Materials:

Clearsnap 'Cosmic Faces'
  style stone
Orange, red, gold and silver
  acrylic paint
Heart feature charm
7.5cm (3in) circle of white cotton
A selection of seed beads
Template B, cut from
  non-woven white medium
  weight interlining

Tools:

Basic tool kit
Paintbrush
Glue

Instructions:

1 Use the orange, red and gold paints to colour the style stone.

2 Using orange, red and silver paint, colour the 7.5cm (3in) circle of cotton and allow to dry.

3 Gather the circle inwards to form the outer frill using tiny running stitches. Manipulate until the gathered circle is approximately 5cm (2in) across.

4 Stitch the style stone on top of the gathers. If the style stone does not cover the stitching tighten the gathering until it does. If the style stone is loose then a small amount of glue may be put on the back to provide a more secure attachment to the cotton.

5 Embellish the cotton circle by sewing on seed beads in groups of three (see detail) with orange thread, then attach the heart feature charm on the lower edge with a string of seed beads as shown.

6 Sew single seed beads round the edge of the circle.

7 Finish by sewing on the medium weight interlining piece and brooch back on to the back of the piece.

Evening Star

More muted colours of paint were used here, emphasising the bright colours of the seed beads. The star charm echoes the star-shaped style stone.

Babouska

Materials:

Template C cut from non- woven
   black medium weight interlining
Template C cut from pink craft felt
Pink 7mm (¼in) sheer ribbon
Bronze sequins and red seed beads
Two arm charms, two leg charms
Artgirlz 'Mini Face' charm

Tools:

Basic tool kit

Instructions:

1 Cut at least thirty lengths of
ribbon, each approximately 6cm
(2¼in) long.

2 Using the needle and pink thread,
sew tiny running stitches along one
edge of a length of ribbon, then
gather it into a rosette.

3 Secure the rosette with a small
stitch and lay to one side. Repeat
on the other ribbons until you
have enough rosettes to cover the
felt template.

4 Sew the face charm into position
on to the felt and then fasten each
rosette in place by stitching on a
sequin with a seed bead in the
centre (see detail).

5 Use a needle and thread to attach
the arms and legs into position on
the body.

6 When complete, stitch or glue
the brooch back to the medium
weight interlining and glue or stitch
the brooch to the back of the body
to finish.

Harlequin
Try using many different ribbons for a multicoloured effect. If you wish, a garter can be made from a length of the ribbon and attached around a leg.

Ikon

Materials:

Sixteen gold beads

Pink, purple, gold, red and turquoise acrylic paint

Two copies of template A cut from non-woven white heavy interlining

Tools:

Basic tool kit

Sizzex hand die-cut system (heart)

Paintbrush

Glue

Instructions:

1 Use the red and gold paints to decorate one side of the first template – gold at the head and red for the body. Allow to dry.

2 Paint the other template with the pink, purple, turquoise and gold paints and allow to dry.

3 Use the die-cutter to cut a heart shape out of the second painted template. Keep the section removed and paint the back and edges in the same colours.

4 Use sharp scissors to cut out a circle from the head of the second template.

5 Glue the two pieces together so that the red and gold parts of the first template show through the holes in the second. When the glue is dry, paint gold around the edges. Allow to dry.

6 Stitch ten gold beads on to the piece around the head (see detail opposite) and attach the punched-out heart with the remaining beads so that it dangles from the bottom of the body.

7 Attach an adhesive brooch back to the piece.

Devotion

Most small die-cut shapes will work with this simple and elegant brooch. Here, a small star is used as an eye-catching design

Mary, Mary By-the-Sea

Materials:

One face charm

Small amount of medium weight iridescent bondable fibre

Metal flakes

Artgirlz 'Crown' charm

Two locks of dyed Wensleydale wool

Twenty-five gold sequins

Gold and blue seed beads

Two drilled shells

Eleven plastic fish beads

Pink, orange, green and blue peel-off marker pens

Template D, cut from non-woven black medium weight interlining

Tools:

Basic tool kit

Iron and ironing board

Instructions:

1 Make a sheet of iridescent bondable fibre by using the manufacturer's instructions, but add in some metal flakes before ironing to give extra sparkle (see detail opposite).

2 Stitch the prepared bondable fibre on to the black medium weight interlining using black thread.

3 Colour the crown with the pink and blue peel-off marker pens, then stitch it into place on top of the prepared piece.

4 Stitch the wool into position as hair.

5 Secure the face charm on top with the needle and thread to disguise the stitching, and then sew on the shell bra.

6 Embellish the lower half of the dress with sequins and beads.

7 Start the fringe by colouring the plastic fish beads with peel-off marker pens. Bring your needle and thread up through the interlining and thread on a sequin, a number of seed beads, a fish bead and a seed bead. Miss out the final seed bead and take the thread back through. Take the needle back down through the interlining to secure the embellishment to the dress.

8 Make ten more fish fringe embellishments and secure them in place.

9 Finish the piece by attaching a brooch back.

Siren Song

This compelling figure has a two-layered fringe to her dress. The shells were coloured with peel-off marker pens to give a vibrant effect.

Nefertiti

Materials:

Gold, light-coloured and dark-coloured metallic seed beads

Artgirlz charms: two 'Little Hand' and two 'Foot'

Template D cut from non-woven white heavy interlining

Two star-shaped beads

Textile glitter pen (black)

Face charm

Tools:

Basic tool kit

Instructions:

1 Colour the surface of the heavy interlining with the glitter pen. This will make any spaces between the beads less obvious.

2 Sew the face charm into position, and secure the two star-shaped beads above and below as shown.

3 Sew on the lighter-coloured metallic beads in circles around the face charm, either singly or in groups of three if you feel confident and want to work more quickly.

4 When the circle reaches the edge of the template sew the darker-coloured metallic beads in lines on to the lower half to form the robe effect, leaving the central area exposed.

5 Sew the hand and feet charms in position. Make sure the feet point in the same direction to give an ancient Egyptian look.

6 Oversew groups of three gold beads (see detail) to the edge to give a rope-like effect to the border.

7 Secure a brooch back to the piece to complete it.

Cleopatra

Turquoise, blue, lilac, black and gold were used on this piece to emphasise the opulent Ancient Egyptian feel.

Miss Milly-Pede

Materials:

Template D cut from non-woven black medium weight interlining
Two 20cm (7¾in) square pieces of sheer nylon
Blue and pink peel-off marker pens
Purple, blue and gold seed beads
Eight assorted shoe charms
Two wooden hand charms
Artgirlz 'Mini Face' charm
Gold acrylic paint

Tools:

Basic tool kit
Medium dry felting needle tool
Paintbrush
Foam block

Instructions:

1 Place the first piece of sheer nylon on to the foam block and distress it with the dry felting needle tool. This creates a very particular rouched effect.

2 Rouche the second piece of nylon and place it on top of the first. Stitch them together using large running stitches in blue thread across the body (see detail opposite).

3 Cut out template D from this newly created fabric and stitch this to the black medium weight interlining templates with blue thread.

4 Position then secure the face charm with the needle and thread. Sew on gold beads around the charm, leaving large loops of beads to represent necklaces.

5 Paint the wooden hand charms with the gold paint. Once dry, take the needle up through the interlining and thread on each hand with three seed beads. Take the needle back down through the hole and secure each time.

6 Colour the shoe charms with peel-off marker pens. Thread one on to your needle along with a number of purple and blue seed beads, and attach to the body shape. Repeat with the other shoe charms.

7 To complete the piece, attach a brooch back.

Purple Janey

Is it possible to have too many shoes? The more you can fit on at the bottom of the piece, the better the effect.

163

Cherokee

Materials:

Template D cut from blue craft felt

Variegated pearl cotton thread

Wooden hand and feet charms

Artgirlz 'Large Face' charm

Template D cut from
  non-woven black medium
  weight interlining

Purple and gold acrylic paint

Fifteen blue beads

Selection of feathers

Tools:

Basic tool kit

Paintbrush

Instructions:

1 Using blanket stitch, stitch all around the edge of the felt template. On the head area add beads on to the stitch to make a 'hairband' of beads.

2 Paint the hand and feet charms with the purple and gold paint, and add gold to the face charm. Allow to dry.

3 Fill the body area with wheels of blanket stitch (see detail).

4 Stitch the face, hand and feet charms on to the body.

5 Glue the feathers into place behind the face.

6 Stitch on the medium weight interlining along with a brooch back to finish.

Twinkletoes

Because feathers are so different from one another, it is easy to make a unique piece, either as a gift or just for your own pleasure.

Micro Macramé Jewellery

by Suzen Millodot

Macramé is a craft where knowing a little lets you create a lot. A macramé knot is not an isolated knot, it is basically the inter-knotting of a few cords to make an imaginative weave, and you can make marvellous jewellery with only one simple knot repeated many times over.

In this chapter, we show you the patterns for two very easy knots, the square knot and the lark's head knot, and how to tie them in different ways with only four cords and combine them with beads to make very stylish necklaces and bracelets.

In the 21st century, macramé has grown up: using delicate, colourful cords and lovely beads, it has once again become fashionable as micro macramé.

The basic tools shown on the right are needed for all the projects. For most of the projects, nylon micro macramé thread or any beading cord, even waxed cord, can be used. All of these are easily available in bead shops or by mail order.

> **Basic tools:**
> Cork place-mat and
>   dressmaker's pins
> Sharp scissors
> Clear nail polish
> Thread zapper (to cut and
>   seal synthetic cords but
>   not silk, wool, cotton
>   or rayon)
> Instant glue gel

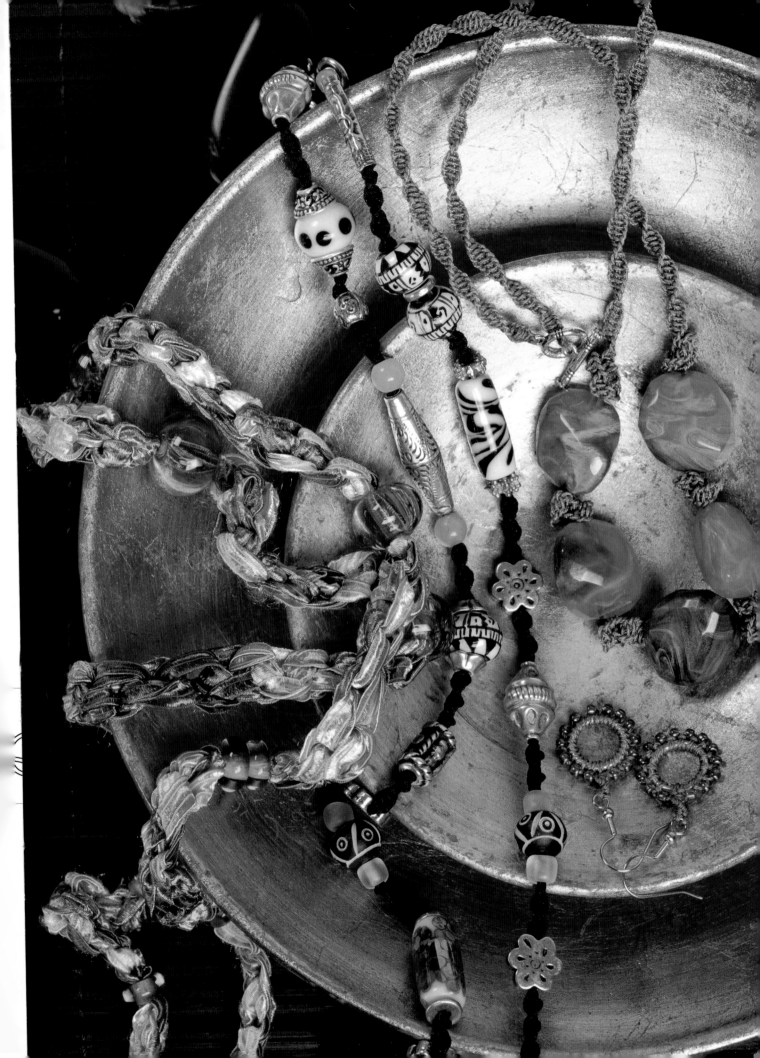

Lampwork Necklace

Materials:

Blue nylon micro macramé thread, 2
pieces: 100cm (39¼in) and
400cm (157½in)

Hook and eye closure

7 lampwork glass beads with
large holes

Finished length:

48cm (19in), including closures

Instructions:

1 'Uncurl' the macramé thread by
wetting it and letting it dry straight – it
dries in minutes. Prepare the ends with
clear nail polish to stiffen them
for threading.

2 Thread both cords halfway through the eye
of the closure, so that the closure sits in the
centre of each. Pin the work to the cork mat.

3 Start to make square knots, using the longer
cords to knot around the shorter 'lazy' cords,
which will not be knotted.

4 When your knotting has reached 12cm (4¾in),
thread a bead on to all four cords.

5 Knot another 2.5cm (1in) of square knots.

6 Add another bead.

7 Continue in this way, adding a larger bead in the
centre (the fourth bead).

8 When you have added 7 beads, knot another
11cm (4³/₈in).

9 Thread the other half of the closure on to the centre (lazy)
cords, 12mm (½in) away from the end of the knotting. Fold
the lazy cords back on themselves and glue down for 12mm
(½in). Cut off the excess with the thread zapper. See the diagram on
the right.

10 Now you have the centre lazy cords secured with glue, continue
using the knotting cords to make square knots for the last 12mm (½in)
until you reach the closure.

11 Cut off the excess cord (see diagram, right) with the thread zapper
and put a spot of instant glue gel on the cut ends to secure them.

Knots used:

Square (see diagram)

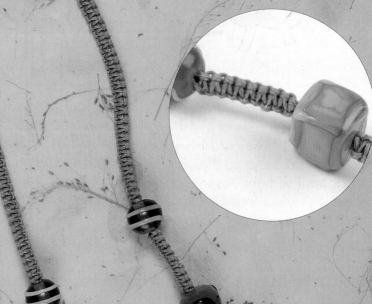

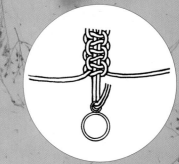

Making a neat finish.

Ethnic Treasure

This version uses the same square knotting technique but with black beading cord and black and ivory coloured beads.

China Blue Necklace

Materials:

Navy blue micro macramé thread,
  2 pieces: 100cm (39¼in) and
  400cm (157½in)

Toggle fastener

9 porcelain Chinese beads with
  large holes

4 small blue beads

Knots used:

Spiral (see right and diagram
H, page 169)

Finished length:

49cm (19in) including
closures

Instructions:

1 Prepare the cords as for the Lampwork Necklace (page 170).

2 Thread both cords halfway through the eye of the closure, so that the closure sits in the centre of each. Pin the work to the cork mat.

3 Start to make spiral knots, using the longer cords to knot around the shorter 'lazy' cords, which will not be knotted.

4 When your knotting has reached 13cm (5in), thread a large bead on to all four cords.

5 Knot another 2.5cm (1in) of spiral knots.

6 Add a large bead, then a small bead, then another large bead.

7 Knot another 2.5cm (1in) of spiral knots.

8 Add a large bead, a small bead, a large bead, a small bead and another large bead.

9 Knot another 2.5cm (1in) of spiral knots.

10 Add a large bead, then a small bead, then another large bead.

11 Make another 12cm (4¾in) of spiral knots.

12 Thread the other half of the closure on to the centre (lazy) cords, 12mm (½in) away from the end of the knotting. Fold the lazy cords back on themselves and glue down for 12mm (½in). Cut off the excess with the thread zapper (see the diagram at the bottom of page 170).

13 Now you have the centre lazy cords secured with glue, continue using the knotting cords to make spiral knots for the last 12mm (½in) until you reach the closure.

14 Cut off the excess cord with the zapper, put a spot of instant glue gel on the cut ends to secure them.

A Passion for Purple

This version, with dark purple micro macramé thread and large purple felt beads has a finished length of 57cm (22½in). You need cords of 130cm (51in) and 500cm (197in) to make it.

Glass Pendant

Materials:

Royal blue nylon satin 1mm cord,
  2 pieces: 100cm (39¼in) and 400cm (157½in)
Toggle fastener
Dichroic glass pendant

Knots used:

Square (see right, top) and
  spiral (see right, bottom
  and H, page 169)

Finished length:

45cm (17¾in) including closures

Instructions:

1 Prepare the cord ends with clear nail polish.

2 Thread both cords halfway through the eye of the closure, so that the closure sits in the centre of each. Pin the work to the cork mat.

3 Start to make square knots, using the longer cords to knot around the shorter 'lazy' cords, which will not be knotted.

4 When your knotting has reached 12cm (4¾in), change to spiral knots for the next 20cm (7¾in).

5 Resume square knotting for the next 11cm (4³/₈in). Add the dichroic glass pendant.

6 Thread the other half of the closure on to the centre (lazy) cords, 12mm (½in) away from the end of the knotting. Fold the lazy cords back on themselves and glue down for 12mm (½in). Cut off the excess with the thread zapper (see the diagram at the bottom of page 170).

7 Now you have the centre lazy cords secured with glue, continue using the knotting cords to make square knots for the last 12mm (½in) until you reach the closure.

8 Cut off the excess cord with the zapper and put a spot of instant glue gel on the cut ends to secure them.

Coconut Creation

Spiral and square knots with black 1mm cotton cord combine with a coconut shell pendant and six etched bone beads to create a beautiful, ethnic-looking necklace. Four pieces of cord are needed, two of 100cm (39¼in) each and two of 400cm (157½in) each. The knotting is started in the centre (so that the knotting cords will be shorter and easier to manage). The pendant is added to the centre of the two longer pieces of cord with a horizontal lark's head knot, and the two shorter pieces are threaded in the centre through the loop of the knot to become the lazy cords. There are now four cords on each side. The beads are added to the knotting when required by threading all four cords through each bead then continuing the knotting. When long enough, the two lazy cords on each side are overlapped and glued, and the knotting is continued over them, making the join practically invisible.

Tassel Earrings

Materials:

Fuchsia nylon micro macramé thread,
 4 pieces: 36cm (14in) each

2 silver earring hooks

2 Celtic star beads

6 No. 6 seed beads

Approx. 160 small seed beads for tassels

Knots used:

Spiral (see right and diagram H, page 169) and overhand (see below)

Finished length:

9.5cm (3¾in), but you can vary this

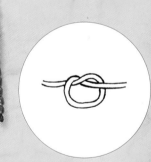

Instructions:

1 Uncurl the cord by wetting then drying it straight. Brush clear nail polish on the cord ends.

2 Thread two pieces of cord through the loop on the earring hook, placing it in the centre of the cords, then fold them in half.

3 Thread a no. 6 seed bead on to the four ends of the cords, moving it up to just below the earring hook.

4 Thread on the star bead and another no. 6 seed bead. Pin the work to the cork mat.

5 Make ten spiral knots (or more if you would like a longer earring).

6 Add another no. 6 seed bead.

7 On each of the four cords, thread seventeen to twenty small seed beads (make each one a different length) to make a tassel.

8 At the end of each cord, make a small overhand knot (see right, top diagram) as close to the last bead as possible. If an overhand knot is too small and goes through the bead hole, you can make a double overhand knot (see right, bottom).

9 Cut off the excess cords with the thread zapper. Seal with a tiny drop of instant glue gel.

10 Repeat from step 1 to make a matching earring.

An overhand knot.

A double overhand knot, useful if a single knot goes through the bead hole.

Chinese Charm

Use blue nylon micro macramé thread, Chinese porcelain beads and blue seed beads to create these lovely oriental earrings.

Spiral Necklace

Materials:

Blue nylon micro macramé thread, 2
   pieces: 200cm (78in) each
Purple nylon micro macramé thread, 2
   pieces: 200cm (78in) each
7 lampwork glass beads
Toggle fastener

Knots used:

Spiral (see right and diagram
H, page 169). Knot from the
centre outwards in order to
work with shorter knotting
cords. By alternating knotting
and lazy cords after each
bead, you change the visible
outer colour.

Finished length:

47cm (18½in)
including closures

Instructions:

1 Prepare the cord by uncurling it, as in previous
projects. Brush clear nail polish on the ends.

2 Thread all four cords through the largest
bead, placing it at the centre of the cords.
Pin the work to the cork mat.

3 Make 4.5cm (1¾in) of spiral knots.

4 Add a bead.

5 Change the knotting and 'lazy' cords and make
another 4.5cm (2in) of spiral knots. The knotting will
now be in the second colour.

6 Add a bead. Change the knotting and 'lazy' cords and
repeat steps 3, 4 and 5 until you have three beads (as well as
the centre bead).

7 Thread the loop half of the closure on to the centre (lazy) cords, 12mm (½in) away from the
end of the knotting. Fold the lazy cords back on themselves and glue down for 12mm (½in).
Cut off the excess with the thread zapper (see the diagram at the bottom of page 170).

8 Now you have the centre lazy cords secured with glue, continue using the knotting
cords to make spiral knots for the last 12mm (½in) until you reach the closure.

9 Cut off the excess cord with the zapper and put a spot of instant glue gel on the cut
ends to secure them.

10 Repeat steps 3 to 9 with the cords on the other side of the centre bead, to finish
the necklace.

Beautiful Bone

This version is made using turquoise and grey micro macramé thread with Chinese etched bone beads and a spiral knot tassel, made in the same way as the earrings on page 176.

Pink Necklace

Materials:

Pink/red novelty knitting yarn,
  2 pieces: 100cm (39¼in) and
  640cm (252in)
5 large beads with large holes
A smaller bead with a very large hole

Tools:

Basic tools plus a 12cm (4¾in)
  piece of fuse wire (to help thread
  the yarn through the beads)

Finished length:

64cm (25¼in)

Instructions:

1 Thread the short piece of yarn
through the centre bead until it is
halfway along. This makes the
lazy cord.

2 Cut the long piece into two pieces.
Thread them through the large bead
until the bead is in the centre of
both pieces.

3 Secure the yarn next to the bead
with a pin, on the side that will not be
knotted yet, to prevent slipping. Pin to
the cork mat.

4 With the short piece of yarn in the middle
(lazy cord), make square knots with the two
longer pieces. Make 8cm (3¼in) of knotting.

5 Add a large bead.

6 Knot another 8cm (3¼in) of square knotting.

7 Add another large bead.

8 Continue knotting for approx. 15cm (6in) or as long as you wish.
Unpin from the cork mat.

9 Turn the work around, remove the anchor pin next to the centre
bead. Repin to the cork mat.

10 Repeat steps 4 to 8 on the other side.

11 Thread the right-hand side of the square knotting through the
smaller bead from right to left.

Knots used:

Square knots, but knotted
around only one lazy cord
(see diagram) as the yarn is
thick. Start in the centre in
order to work with shorter
length knotting cords.

180

10 Gather the four cords together in a pleasing combination (if you need to, you can move any bead slightly to the left or right by moving the knots). Add a bead spacer at each end of the knotting (or if not using bead spacers, make an overhand knot with all four cords, as shown in the design below). Pin the work to the cork mat at the junction of all four cords.

11 On one side, make 6cm (2³/₈in) of square knotting using the longer cords as the knotting cords. Add the toggle fastener and make a neat finish in the same way as in steps 9 to 11 on page 170.

12 Finish the other side in the same way as in step 11.

Coral Gold

Use Celtic pewter beads with red glass and coral beads and orange and gold seed beads to make this gorgeous necklace.

Chinese Rings

Materials:

1mm Chinese knotting
  cord, 1 piece: 96cm
  (37¾in) long

Flat, fused glass bead
  with large hole

Knots used:

Square (see diagram)

Instructions:

1 Stiffen cord ends with clear nail polish.

2 Fold the piece of cord in half and thread it through the bead.

3 Arrange it so that it goes around your finger (or the future wearer's finger) once, slightly loose, with an overlap of 5mm (¼in).

4 Put a couple of spots of instant glue gel on the overlapping join to secure it. Pull it backwards through the bead so that the join is inside the hole and does not show. Pin the work to the cork mat.

5 With the remaining long ends of the cord, make square knots around the fixed ring of cords. Make sure the knots are tightly woven and as close together as possible, to make the ring fairly stiff.

6 To finish, cut the free ends of the knotting and seal them with the thread zapper as close to the knotting as possible.

7 Put a spot of instant glue gel on each end to secure them.

Heavenly Blue

Choose cord colours to bring out the beauty of your bead. This bright blue looks striking with the iridescent sheen in the bead.

Scalloped Bracelet

Materials:

Purple 1mm satin cord, 2 pieces:
  50cm (19¾in) and 180cm (70¾in)
Approx. 108 no. 6 seed beads
Toggle fastener

Knots used:

Vertical lark's head knots around central lazy cords, alternating left and right sides (see diagram right), and square knots (see diagram far right)

Finished length:

22cm (8¾in)

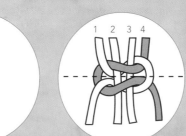

Instructions:

1 Stiffen cord ends with clear nail polish.

2 Thread both cords through the loop end of the toggle until they are both centrally placed at the toggle.

3 Fold them down and pin on to the cork mat to start knotting. Make one square knot with the longer cords around the shorter cords.

4 Thread three beads on to the left cord.

5 Make a vertical lark's head knot with the left cord around the two central cords.

6 Thread three beads on to the right cord.

7 Make a vertical lark's head knot with the right cord around the two central cords.

8 Continue adding beads and knotting until you reach 1.25cm (½in) before the length you require.

9 Thread the toggle fastener on to the central cords.

10 Finish in exactly the same way as in the Lampwork Necklace on page 170, by cutting and glueing down the lazy cords and continuing knotting over them, finishing with a square knot.

Beaded Beauty

This alternative uses dark red Chinese knotting cords and coral and gold seed beads for a subtle but sumptuous effect.

Sea-Green Earrings

Materials:

Green nylon micro macramé thread, two pieces: 66cm (26in) each

Two earring hooks

Two turquoise jump rings 12mm (½in) in diameter

28 to 30 seed beads

Knots used:

Vertical lark's head around the ring (right) and spiral (see right, below and diagram H, page 169)

Finished length:

4cm (1½in)

Instructions:

1 Prepare the cords by wetting them then drying them straight to take out the unwanted curl (the thread dries in minutes). Stiffen the ends with clear nail polish.

2 Leave about 12.5cm (5in) of cord free before tying a vertical lark's head knot (see the top diagram) in the right direction towards the centre of the ring.

3 Add a seed bead, then tie another vertical lark's head knot below the first, in the same direction.

4 Repeat step 3, adding a bead before each new knot until you have gone all around the ring and reached the beginning again.

5 Decide how long you wish the spiral knotting to be between the ring and the earring hook, for example I wanted 8mm (¼in), then thread the two cords through the loop of the earring hook, 8mm (¼in) away from the ring. Pin to the cork mat.

6 Fold the free ends over the loop of the earring hook. Cut them 8mm (¼in) and glue them down exactly as in steps 9, 10 and 11 on page 170.

7 Make spiral knots around the centre cord back down to the ring. Cut and seal the ends and secure them with a dot of instant glue gel.

8 Repeat steps 2 to 7 to make the second earring.

Perfect Pink

These earrings were made in the same way but with silver jump rings and seed beads and dark pink micro macramé thread.

Lavender Necklace

Materials:

Lavender Chinese 1mm knotting cord, 2 pieces: 210cm (82¾in) each

Toggle (or hook and eye) closure

Approx. 72 no. 6 seed beads

Finished length:

48cm (19in) including closures

Knots used:

Crossover square knots: interchanging knotting and lazy cords after each knot (see diagram below)

Instructions:

1 Prepare the ends of the cords with clear nail polish.

2 Thread the two cords through the loop of the closure until the halfway point of the cords.

3 Pin to the cork mat to start knotting. Make one square knot.

4 Bring the outside cords into the centre, to become the lazy cords.

5 With the previously lazy cords now on the outside, use them to tie another square knot. The knotting will look lacy.

6 Repeat steps 4 and 5 until the knotting is 6.5cm (2½in) long.

7 Add a bead on to each outside cord before bringing them to the centre to become the lazy cords.

8 Use the cords that are now on the outside to make a square knot, as before.

9 Repeat steps 7 and 8 for another 30cm (11¾in).

10 Resume knotting without beads, as in steps 4 and 5, until another 5.5cm (2¼in) has been knotted.

11 Add the other half of the closure, threading it on to the centre lazy cords.

12 Cut, trim and glue down following steps 9, 10 and 11 on page 170.

Precious Pearls

Black cord and pearl and clear seed beads make this a striking alternative.

Publisher's Note

If you would like more books on jewellery, try the following:

Ornamental Knots for Beaded Jewellery by Suzen Millodot, Search Press, 2008
Woven Crystal Beaded Jewellery by Céline Marchand, Search Press, 2007
80 Original Charms by Martine Routier, Search Press, 2007
Crystal Beaded Jewellery by Christine and Sylvie Hooghe, Search Press, 2005
Beginner's Guide to Beading on a Loom by Alexandra Kidd, Search Press, 2005